Be the Leader
Make the Difference
Second Edition

The Three C Leadership Model

Paul B. Thornton

Griffin Publishing Group
Torrance, California

Editor: PeopleSpeak

Director of Operations: Robin L. Howland

Project Manager: Bryan K. Howland

Book and Cover Design: m2design group

10 9 8 7 6 5 4 3 2 1

ISBN 1-58000-091-6

Griffin Publishing Group
www.griffinpublishing.com
1-800-472-9741

Manufactured in the United States of America
Printed by QUESTprint

DEDICATION

To Mary Jean, my wife and
favorite leadership discussion partner,
and our wonderful children—
Kate and Andrew.

To my mentors and teachers—
Paul Hersey, Roy Masters,
Bill Huber, and Tom Peters.

CONTENTS

TOP 10 RESOURCES
NEW THINKING FOR LEADERS

Be The Leader, Make The Difference
Reviewed by Tom Brown

Some of the best concepts in management have been captured via a sweet-and-simple model: just think of McKinsey's 7-S model. Thornton, who believes "that leaders provide their followers with something they can't provide themselves," also believes fervently that a "3 C" model effectively captures the fundamental role of leadership. At various times, "people need help in seeing what's possible (Challenge), Confidence to take action, and Coaching in how to proceed. Effective leaders serve others and provide what's needed to help grow and develop." Thus, Thornton's book becomes a kind of manual for leaders who are looking for a direct, straightforward, clear-as-glass view of leadership. Much to his credit, given the goal of his book, Thornton does not try to wax eloquent, deal in eloquent, deal in nuances, or explore all the subtleties of leadership. And, although he does not do this, almost all of his chapters could end in exclamation points; Thornton revels in giving leaders the kind of direct imparatives which can cut through the daily clutter of most business executives' lives. So, whether it's "Ask Challenging Questions" or "Make People Think For Themselves," Thornton hones each chapter to a single thrust, one which no reader could misunderstand—or dodge. **Be The Leader** *is a powerful book, one which deserves wide readership for his graceful simplicity and urgent appeal to stop managing and start leading—really leading!*

ENDORSEMENTS

"I love the book. It is a book that I will keep returning to time and time again. It is the next best thing to having a leadership coach at your side."

—Joe Malone,
Entrepreneur and Director, Business Development
jenzabar.com

"You can't have great customer service without great leaders. I love Paul Thornton's book, *Be the Leader, Make the Difference.*"

—Stew Leonard, Jr.
President and CEO
Stew Leonard's, World's Largest Dairy Store

"Paul Thornton handles the theory and practice of leadership with clear, concise, and current concepts. An easy-to-read book that can be used in any work setting or seminar on leadership and by the CEO and the manager at all levels within an organization. I found the chapters on vision and challenge particularly relevant for our competitive global environment of today.

I will use the Three C Model of Leadership throughout our organization in the coming year to provide focus and inspiration in accomplishing our goals."

—Dr. Carol A. Leary, President
Bay Path College

"Leadership is an art, as it is constantly evolving in step with business. One-size programs don't fit all situations. The Three C Leadership Model provides the nuts and bolts of good management with enough examples to offer 'real world' approaches."

—Ronald Coburn, Chairman and CEO
Savage Arms, Inc.

"Thornton has a special ability to coordinate fresh ideas that empower managers with the insight and skills required by the ever-changing demands of Corporate America."

—Anthony F. Assante
Allmerica Investments, Inc.

"Leadership, more than ever, is required in all organizations. Paul's text, more than most, provides a practical, succinct, easy-to-understand leadership model and valuable guidance on how to develop your leadership skills."

—Mike Peterson, Acting Dean
School of Business Administration
American International College

"*Be the Leader, Make the Difference* provides the right ingredients to produce effective leaders. It's required reading for anyone who wants to lead and add value."

—Steve Davis, President
American Saw & Manufacturing

PART I
Introduction

"Leaders needed." Today's competitive and demanding business world requires people throughout an organization to step up and take on a leadership role. I believe everyone has untapped leadership abilities.

A lot has been written about leadership behaviors such as creating a vision, gaining alignment, empowering, benchmarking, motivating, coaching, and mentoring. But what's missing? Leaders need a way to fit the pieces together. For example, how does creating a vision relate to coaching or empowerment? My **3-C Leadership Model** (challenge, confidence, coaching, see figure 1), provides a framework that helps leaders know what to do, how to do it, and when to do it. This model explains how the leadership pieces fit together into a unified whole.

My basic premise is that leaders provide their followers with something they can't provide themselves. If people always knew what to do, they wouldn't need leaders. Unfortunately, that's not the case. At various times, people need help in seeing what's possible, confidence to take action, and coaching in how to proceed. Effective leaders provide what's needed to help people grow and develop.

Leaders have to know their followers—their abilities, dreams, frustrations, skills, talents, and weaknesses. Leaders can't be isolated or constantly busy. They need to get out of their offices and talk with people, ask questions, listen, and see people in action. The best leaders are constantly trying to find out what people need to be more effective and successful. Their attitude is "How can I help?" not "What am I going to get out of it?"

Leadership requires someone who has the desire and willingness to initiate action, make decisions, and take risks others don't want to face.

Be the Leader, Make the Difference challenges you to step up and take on a leadership role. By challenging people, building their confidence, and coaching them to succeed, leaders make the difference.

The following chapters describe in greater detail my research on what effective leaders do, and the skills needed to implement the **3-C Leadership Model**.

- Part I describes the **3-C Leadership Model**. It explains what leaders do in performing each of their key roles. The relationships among challenge, confidence, and coaching are also discussed.

- Part II provides a more in-depth discussion of various techniques leaders can use to challenge people. For each technique a step-by-step formula is provided. The section summary describes a number of well known leaders who stepped forward and challenged the status quo.

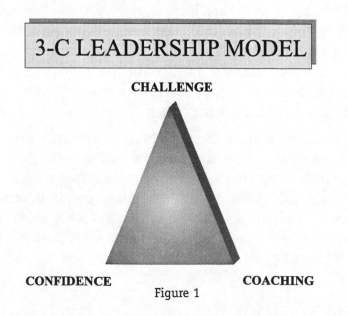

Figure 1

- Part III explains various approaches leaders use to build confidence in their associates. Numerous "how to" examples are included to point out the techniques used by successful leaders.The section summary explains what some famous leaders have done to build confidence in their followers.

- Part IV further describes when and how leaders perform the role of coach and teacher. Stories and examples are used to highlight how the best leader/coaches help people achieve maximum performance. The section summary highlights some world-class coaches.

- Part V discusses the need to lead by setting examples. It also describes the desire and skills leaders need to help people succeed.

- Part VI identifies resources to help you develop your leadership skills.

Leaders provide the challenge, confidence, and coaching people need to achieve their best performance.

—Paul B. Thornton

CHAPTER 1
3-C Leadership Model

Leaders don't all look and act the same. Some are tall, others short. Some are passionate and intense; others are low-key and quiet. Some are brilliant; others have average IQs. What, then, are the characteristics shared by most leaders?

One common thread is that leaders help followers grow, develop, and achieve their best performance. Leaders intervene when people need help. For example, people sometimes need help in situations like the following:

- Seeing what's possible in the future

- Facing reality and dealing with difficult choices

- Finding courage to deal with adversity

- Defining and solving problems

- Developing new strategies and learning new skills

- Working together as a team

In situations like these, a leader must do whatever is necessary to help the individual or team move forward.

The Army's motto—"Be All That You Can Be" is both simple and powerful. Leaders help people achieve that goal. In essence, leaders do three things:

- They challenge people.

- They build people's confidence.

- They coach people.

By providing the right C (challenge, confidence, or coaching), leaders help people become more and achieve more than they thought possible.

The three Cs are interrelated. As leaders coach and mentor people, they feel more prepared, more confident. As confidence increases, people are more willing to take on bigger and bigger challenges. Sue Lewis, executive vice president and chief real estate officer, The Travelers, states, "Many leaders are good at only one or two Cs but not all three. In today's business world challenge is common. However coaching and building confidence are frequently missing."

Desire to Lead

What gives people the desire to lead? People's values and beliefs are often shaped by significant emotional events. These defining moments energize some people to take a stand against injustice or pursue a new standard of excellence. In other instances, the desire to lead is sparked by a compelling vision. "My vision gets me excited. My adrenaline starts pumping." Desire to lead may be generated simply by the desire to help others grow and blossom. An executive states, "Somewhere along the way I learned it was very exciting and rewarding to help other people achieve their dreams. That's what leaders do."

If a person lacks "desire," he or she will not take on a leadership role. Charlie Eitel, former president and COO, Interface,Inc. states, "To want to be the leader is to risk failure. I'm convinced that everyone is afraid to fail—it's a matter of degree. Fear is what causes people to 'play not to lose.'" On the other hand, seeing what is possible and playing to win is exciting and energizing.

Challenge

Why do leaders need to challenge the status quo? All of us have "comfort zones" in which we like to operate. In our comfort zones, we understand our roles and responsibilities. We know the rules and regulations. In addition, we know how to be successful. The word "comfort" is very telling—it means feeling safe and secure about something that is known and predictable. People often set goals and objectives in or close to their comfort zones. For example, "Last year we had 4.4 inventory turns; let's shoot for 4.7 this year." [Inventory turns indicate the number of times during a given year that a company turned over or sold its average inventory.] In addition, when confronted with information that says "You must change!" many people deny or rationalize that information and, in essence, cling to their comfort zones.

Comments like "Don't rock the boat" or "But this is the way we've always done it" are saying, "I want to stay in my comfort zone." But today, you must make waves, reinvent, reengineer, innovate, and try something new and different if you want to be successful. Today the message is "Get out of your comfort zone to succeed."

T. J. Rodgers, the founder and CEO of Cypress Semiconductor, is a strong decisive leader who forces himself and his employees to frequently leave their comfort zones. He has this quote on his office wall: "Be Realistic—Demand the Impossible." Why demand the impossible? The simple answer is the marketplace requires constant change and constant improvement. Demanding the impossible forces people to rethink what they do, how they do it, and why they do it. For example, if you had to double your productivity in the next six months, what would you do? Chances are you couldn't do it by simply working harder. You would have to work smarter and find innovative ways to double your output.

In the past, managers were taught to set goals that were "challenging but attainable," which means close to the comfort zone. Impossible goals, on the other hand, are significantly outside the comfort zone. In today's globally competitive business world, individuals and teams are often asked to achieve impossible goals. They aren't being asked to make just a 2 to 3 percent improvement; it's more likely to be a 30 to 50 percent improvement. For example, members of a design team at the Hamilton Standard Division of United Technologies Corporation told me they recently had to cut their cycle time from 12 months to 3 months. [Cycle time refers to the length of time it takes to complete a process such as designing a part or paying a bill.]

In this constant-improvement environment, the plateaued employee who's unwilling to leave his or her comfort zone isn't going to succeed. The person who's coasting or has a business-as-usual-attitude will not survive. All employees must accept change and experiment with new and innovative ways of working. Today, you can't plateau; you must keep your skills up-to-date. If you're not adding new tools to your toolbox and constantly finding ways to improve your product and service, you won't be able to satisfy demanding customers.

Ways To Challenge

When you see people stuck in their comfort zones—in their thinking, attitudes, or behavior—you need to step forward and provide a challenge. Help people understand why change is needed and what new performance standards are required. Effective leaders are able to clearly and succinctly explain the marketplace demands driving the need for improved performance.

Actress, Cicely Tyson, says that challenges make you discover aspects of yourself that you never knew existed. Challenges are what make people stretch and go beyond the norm. Leaders use many of the following approaches to challenge people and change the status quo:

- **Describing their vision—** Every leader has one. Visions describe a future that's better in some important way. A clear and compelling vision challenges people to think and act differently as they pursue a new agenda.

- **Establishing stretch goals—** When Richard Davis became CEO of Rand McNally, the company launched an average of ten new products per year. He challenged the organization to launch 120 new products during his first year. Nothing commands people's attention like demanding targets and timetables.

- **Asking provocative questions—** Leaders often ask "why" and "what if," questions. The right questions force people to examine underlying assumptions and consider new possibilities. Stuart Hornery, retired chairman, Lend Lease Corporation states, "Every project we take starts with a question—how can we do what's never been done before?"

- **Benchmarking—** Ayn LaPlant, president, Beekley Corporation states, "Benchmarking is another way we challenge people. I want our employees to look at other companies and find best practices. If you're really committed to continuous improvement, you have a natural curiosity to learn from the best."

- **New assignments—** Ruth Branson, senior vice president, Shaw's Supermarkets states, "We challenge people through cross-fertilization. We move people into new positions, from one function to another, from line to staff, from a district to the corporate office. These job changes stretch people to see the business from new perspectives."

All of these leadership actions—stating your vision, establishing stretch goals, asking tough questions, benchmarking and new assignments—challenge people to see bigger possibilities and pursue bigger goals. Leaders also set the example by challenging themselves. If the leader isn't getting out of his comfort zone, it's unlikely others will follow.

Success Versus Failure

Assume you challenged an individual or team that then achieved success. What happens when you're successful? First, other people benchmark *your* operation. They study what you do, imitate what you do, and very quickly become as good as you are. Standing still, staying in your comfort zone, is suicidal.

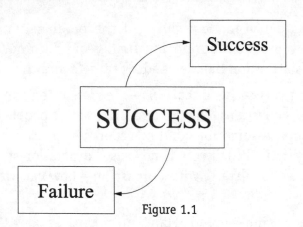

Figure 1.1

A second aspect of success is that you lose your motivation to change. People's attitude becomes "Why change? I've been successful." It's difficult to change behavior if current tactics are working. After achieving success, many people begin to ease up. The history of business suggests that market leaders often get arrogant, complacent, and then very conservative, but being very conservative in a rapidly changing world is a recipe for disaster. Success often breeds failure. (See figure 1.1.) If you were to look at the 1980 list of Fortune 500 companies, you would find that over 40 percent have gone out of business. Some failed slowly; some didn't even realize they were failing until it was too late.

Some companies, teams, and individuals, however, keep amassing one success after another. How do they do it? I believe they keep challenging themselves. They keep challenging themselves, even after achieving success. On the basis of extensive interviews, Charles Garfield claims that one of the distinguishing characteristics of successful people is that they avoid their comfort zones and constantly seek higher levels of accomplishment. Successful leaders such as Jack Welch, Lawrence Bossidy, Andy Grove, and Roger Enrico are constantly challenging their organizations to do more and do it better and faster.

NBA (National Basketball Association) Coach Pat Riley says that in sports, those players who keep winning and breaking records are the ones who keep doing inner research. They keep developing new attitudes and different ideas about what it takes to exceed their best performance, to go above and beyond.

My motto is "Continuous challenge produces continuous improvement...." (see figure 1.2). The challenge is the triggering event. One of my colleagues states, "The challenge is the stimulus that produces a response aimed at improving results." This principle applies to individuals, teams, and organizations. Wolfgang Schmidt, CEO of Rubbermaid, says that to keep organizations on the leading edge, it's critical to offer constant challenge. The challenge is what energizes people to work smarter, harder, and in many cases differently. A tough challenge forces people to find hidden talents, abilities, and motivation.

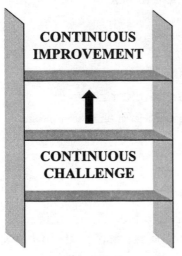

Figure 1.2

Summary—Challenge

One of the most satisfying aspects of being a leader is that you help people become more and achieve more than they ever thought possible. Leaders stretch people beyond the boundaries they had set for themselves. A major way they do this is through the challenges they present . Former Secretary of State Henry Kissinger says that every executive has the responsibility to make his or her associates do what they did not know they could do. You do them a favor by challenging them and insisting on standards they would otherwise brush aside. Try answering these leadership questions:

1. Do you set the example? Do you challenge yourself to leave your own comfort zone?

2. Are you willing to be demanding and set high standards?

3. Are you willing to challenge people even after they have achieved success?

Leaders set high standards, and often expect more than others think is possible. They often believe that people have untapped skills and abilities. A senior executive states, "Leaders don't expect people to 'hit the wall.' They believe people are capable of ongoing improvement in everything they do."

Doing It Right the First Time
Means You're Staying in Your Comfort Zone

—sign on the desk of a human resources manager of a large aerospace company

Confidence

The second variable of the **3-C Leadership Model** is confidence. Being confident means having a strong belief and faith in one's abilities and motivation.

When teams and individuals face challenging goals that are significantly outside their comfort zones, what happens to their confidence? It drops. It's not unusual to hear comments such as, "There is no way we can meet that schedule" or "There is no way we can cut costs by 40 percent." Moving outside one's comfort zone is scary and uncomfortable. In addition, a demanding challenge produces stress. This often impacts people's ability to learn the very skills that will help them improve their performance. One of my colleagues states, "People who lack confidence spend a lot of time hesitating and second-guessing. Decisions tend to be put off or not made."

When people lose their self-confidence or lack the confidence they need to deal with a tough challenge, a leader must emerge and take the necessary steps to restore or build their confidence.

Effective leaders make people believe that they have what it takes— that they can compete and succeed. Sometimes people need to hear a voice that says, "I believe in you—you can do it."

However, confidence and self-esteem come with a catch. People must earn them. Some experts recommend the use of affirmations. I don't. Repeating an affirmation to yourself, such as "I am confident I can face any situation," doesn't make it true. If it were true, why would you have to repeat it twenty times a day, seven days a week? Real confidence is based on hard work and accomplishments. Having up-to-date knowledge and skills, learning from success and failure, overcoming obstacles, and achieving goals are the building blocks of confidence. People must deserve to feel confident.

Focus on the Positive

How do you build confidence? Let me describe two scenarios and then make some comparisons.

When my son, Andrew, was in the eighth grade, he brought home these interim grades: five As, three Bs, and one C. What grade do you think I focused on? The C. I gave Andy "the lecture": "Andrew, you need to study harder, be more focused in class, do your homework more carefully, etc." By the time I finished, you would have thought he had flunked out of the eighth grade! I'm sorry to say I think he felt like a failure, and that was obviously *not* what I was trying to accomplish.

The second scenario involves Sam Walton, the founder of Wal-Mart Stores. Long before benchmarking was in vogue, Sam was out visiting his competitors, studying what they did, and borrowing their good ideas. On one trip, Sam and one of his vice presidents visited a store that was very poorly run. It was dirty, the people who worked there weren't customer focused, and the merchandise was poorly displayed. As Sam and his vice president walked back to their car, Sam said, "Did you notice in aisle four what a *terrific job* they are doing merchandising their sporting goods equipment?"

Sam Walton found and focused on the one positive aspect of the store. I, on the other hand, focused on the one negative part of Andy's grades. When you think about it, a C in a course really isn't that negative.

The first rule in building confidence is this: Focus on the positive—focus on what people can do and are doing. As a middle manager states, "Notice effort and results. Acknowledge what's working, what's changing, what's improving." As Ken Blanchard has said, "Catch people doing something right." Too often we focus most of our time on negatives—problems, mistakes, errors. Little if any time is spent on the positives, the successes, the accomplishments.

For example, if you receive survey results that tell you 93 percent of your customers are satisfied, what do you do? Do you do additional research to find out what makes 93 out of 100 customers happy? Or do you focus all your efforts on finding out why those 7 are unhappy? The issue is a matter of balance. Certainly you have to deal with problems and unhappy customers, but don't overlook all the positive work that is being done. Focusing on positive skills and accomplishments helps build confident employees. In their book, *Leaders*, Warren Bennis and Bert Nanus identify several factors that mark superb leaders. At the top of the list is that they don't focus on weaknesses, they build on strengths. That includes their own strengths as well as the positive attributes and strengths of their followers.

Confidence Versus Fear

The opposite of confidence is fear. When people are motivated by fear, they don't take risks or show initiative. Rather, they wait to be told what to do, and then they do just that and no more. That's not going to make them or their company successful in the marketplace. A president and CEO of a Fortune 100 company stated, "I think we have too much fear at our company. And fear manifests itself in many ways—in defensiveness, in committees, in endless and exhaustive studies, and in redone studies—all because we are worried and afraid." Fear is not only costly and time consuming, but it also inhibits creativity and innovation. Judith Bardwick, author of *Danger in the Comfort Zone*, says that in organizations where people are scared, the ratio of "yes people" rises exponentially in relation to the level of fear. People who lack confidence avoid expressing their true feelings and only try to placate those in power. Today business organizations need confident people to face and deal with some very difficult challenges. Effective leaders know that when people have fears and doubts about their abilities, their performance is lackluster at best. On the other hand, leaders know that confident people face a tough challenge with the attitude "I'll find a way to be successful. I have what it takes."

Here are some actions leaders take to build confidence in their associates:

- **Affirm people's talents—** Don Sweet, vice-president, finance, Siebe Pneumatics states, "People need self-confidence or belief in themselves so that they can perform with the best. I sometimes simply affirm my confidence in people. For example, one of our sales reps was facing a new, very demanding account. I said to him, I know you can do this. I know you can get through to this client."

- **Rewarding and recognizing accomplishments—** Real confidence is based on achieving results, one success after another. When leaders provide rewards and recognition, it's a validation of people's talents and determination.

- **Training and development—** Bill Cox, vice president, human resources, Ahlstrom Corporation states, "We build people's confidence by making sure all employees receive ongoing training. One of our key beliefs is that competence builds confidence."

- **Empower people—** Ralph Stayer, former CEO of Johnsonville Foods, built confidence in his workforce by transferring total responsibility and ownership to the people doing the work. When leaders give people responsibility and real authority, they're saying—"I have confidence in you."

- **Remind people of their previous successes**— Sometimes people forget or overlook their previous successes. Jim Ligotti, global product manager, Carrier Corporation states, "When challenges seem overwhelming or when people are reluctant to change, I go back to their successes in non-work related areas. I remind people that they did achieve success in other areas of their life."

All of these leadership actions—affirming people, recognizing accomplishments, skills training, empowering people, and reminding them of previous successes—have a significant impact on people's self-confidence. Confident people face reality and have a "can do" attitude. Leaders also need a healthy amount of their own self-confidence. Confident leaders aren't afraid to attack "sacred cows," make tough decisions, and candidly communicate their position.

Summary—Confidence

Think about how Rick Pitino builds confidence. He has coached basketball at the college and professional levels. At the beginning of each season, Rick meets with his team. He doesn't start by talking about the tough, demanding schedule. Rather, he starts by talking about his players—their skills, abilities, and attitudes. He reminds them of their previous accomplishments and how effective they were when they worked as a team. He makes them believe they can compete successfully against any and all competition. In essence, he builds their confidence first, then he talks about the tough, demanding schedule ahead of them.

In business, leaders need to use that approach but often don't. Too often in business, managers and leaders immediately fixate on the challenge. For example, comments like these are common:

"We have a crisis. We must reinspect all hardware by the end of the month" or "Unless we reduce cost and significantly improve quality, we can't compete." Leaders often do little, if anything, to build people's confidence first before such pronouncements. Yet confidence is a very important requirement for achieving success. Top coaches and leaders know that only confident people will readily face and deal with tough challenges. People lacking confidence want to put their heads in the sand and stand still.

Confidence is what separates risk-takers from tree huggers.
—handwritten note posted above the desk of the owner of a small public relations company

Coaching

Thus far I have described the relationship between challenging people and building their confidence. The third variable of the **3-C Leadership Model** is coaching.

Coaching involves helping individuals and teams raise their performance. The best coaches do three things: First, they challenge people to perform at a higher level. They raise the bar of acceptable performance. They establish a culture of continuous improvement. Second, good coaches demonstrate great confidence in people's ability to improve. Their unwavering attitude is "I know you can do it." Third, coaches provide advice and instruction regarding not only what to do but also how to do it. They also provide valuable feedback that helps people improve performance and fine-tune their skills. In essence, good coaches do all three Cs— Challenge, Build Confidence, and Coach—in the coaching process.

Effective leaders/coaches also help people see the big picture. They connect day-to-day learning events with the company's mission, vision, and key strategies. They give people assignments that broaden their understanding of how all pieces of the business puzzle fit together. These assignments and special projects provide opportunities to gain new insights and skills.

In my leadership seminars, I've asked participants to identify behaviors that describe the best coaches in business. Comments have included:

- "Took time to find out what motivated me."
- "Didn't give me all the answers but asked the right questions."
- "Expert on the material. Great credibility."
- "Very approachable."
- "Crafted challenging developmental assignments."
- "Followed up to see how things were going."
- "Provided frequent and precise feedback."
- "After major events, always held 'lesson learned' meetings."

Many leaders spend time in the classroom formally presenting their ideas on management, leadership, and other business topics. For example, Ray Kurlak, former president of the Hamilton Standard Division of United Technologies Corporation, regularly gave one-hour presentations to groups of middle managers on the benefits of team leadership. The two years prior to Roger Enrico's becoming CEO of PepsiCo, he devoted more than four months to coaching and mentoring the next generation of PepsiCo leaders. He created his own leadership course and presented it ten times.

Effective leaders also treat staff meetings and strategy sessions as an opportunity to coach and teach. One of my former bosses used techniques such as

- giving mini-lectures,
- asking probing questions,
- linking events and metrics, and
- facilitating group discussions.

One of my colleagues stated, "His staff meetings are like getting an advanced M.B.A. degree."

Leaders use a variety of approaches to coach people including the following:

- **Create coaching opportunities—** Take the time to carefully observe people as they run meetings, make presentations, and interact with customers. Dan Kelly, vice president, transportation business, International Fuel Cells, gives his staff frequent opportunities to make presentations. He states, "These can be emotional events and powerful learning opportunities." Leaders look for "teachable moments" when people are most open to learning.

- **Show them what great performance looks like—** Top leaders are constantly searching for best practices and great performance in all aspects of business. Encouraging others to observe and study what top performers do and don't do is an excellent coaching technique.

- **Ask questions—** Socrates' basic method of teaching was asking questions. The right questions help people focus on the areas needing improvement. Leaders spend time identifying the best questions to ask such as: "What question will help this person face reality?" "What question will energize this person?" "What question will help this individual identify specific next steps to be taken?"

- **Provide feedback—** Michael Z. Kay, president and CEO, LSG Sky Chefs, Inc. states, "Give frequent, candid feedback. Let people know where they are strong but also where they need to improve. Always demonstrate your confidence in people's ability to learn and grow." He also believes in establishing rigorous consequences, penalties for not taking risks, and trying new ways of getting things done.

- **Set the example—** Great coaches are usually great students. They keep learning and growing throughout their lives. Janice Deskus, vice president, training and quality implementation, CIGNA Health Care states, "Every meeting I attend, I try to walk away with at least one new idea."

Coaches help athletes develop the required skills and mind-set needed to excel in their sport. In a similar way, leaders coach and help people achieve their best performance. These coaching actions—pointing out examples of top performance, asking the right questions, providing helpful feedback and setting a positive example—help people develop the knowledge and skills needed to succeed. Leaders view every coaching event as an opportunity to gain new insights about themselves and their associates.

Summary—Coaching

Dr. W. Edwards Deming was a world-class expert in quality systems and statistical process control. He consulted and taught his techniques to business leaders throughout the world. During his career he often had graduate students working with him. This was a tremendous opportunity to be taught and mentored by the expert in the field. In writing to new graduate students who would be working with him, Dr. Deming always ended each letter with the following statement, "I'm sure I have a lot to learn from you." Dr. Deming's approach reveals an important lesson: The best coaches and teachers look at every coaching situation not only as an opportunity to teach but also as an opportunity to learn. They play the dual roles of teacher and student. In every coaching situation, the teacher has an opportunity to gain new insights and greater understanding. The best leaders know that lifelong learning applies equally to them.

**The human mind, once stretched to a new idea,
never goes back to its original dimension.**

—Oliver Wendell Holmes

3-C Relationships

There are important relationships between the three variables. For example, as leaders coach people they feel more prepared, more confident. As confidence increases, people are willing to take on bigger and bigger challenges.

Figure 1.3 provides a graphic view of another relationship. The line represents a perfect balance between confidence and challenge. According to Mihaly Csikszentmihalyi, professor of psychology and education at the University of Chicago, people on the line are in what he calls a "flow state." In this state people become totally absorbed in what they are doing. Intense focus and concentration are common. People may spend hours on a task, but to them it seems like minutes.

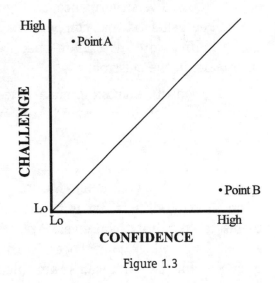

Figure 1.3

However, most of the time there is an imbalance between confidence and challenge. For example, point A represents a person who has little confidence, but faces a big challenge. Training and coaching are required. Or maybe the person needs to be assigned a different task. Point B represents a person who has high confidence, but faces an easy goal. This person needs to be assigned a bigger challenge.

Bill Cox, former vice president of human resources for Dexter Corporation, states, "The 3 Cs (challenge, confidence, coaching) are inseparable. All three are important. At Dexter, we challenge people by assigning them to project teams that have specific deliverables. In addition, our performance management process challenges each employee to achieve specific goals. We build people's confidence by making sure all employees receive ongoing training. For example, all supervisors, working leaders, and managers attend the Zenger Miller Frontline training program and a supervisory certification curriculum. The topics covered include interviewing, running effective meetings, manufacturing practices, quality tools, diversity, finance, and government regulations. One of our key beliefs is that competence builds confidence. Most of the coaching we do is one-on-one. We help people apply what they learn in the classroom.

The 3 Cs constitute a basic formula for leadership success. A balanced combination of challenge, confidence, and coaching is needed."

Conclusion—3-C Leadership Model

The first job of a leader is to understand what individuals or teams can't do for themselves. Are they stuck in their comfort zones? Do they lack confidence? Do they need additional skills to be successful? Effective leaders are able to ask questions that focus on strengths, weaknesses, and obstacles that are holding people back. Leaders know how to get this information without making the individuals or teams feel interrogated or defensive. Effective leaders then provide what's needed. It may be coaching to build skills, it may be actions aimed at building confidence, or it may be a compelling challenge.

Leaders often engage in all three efforts (challenge, confidence, and coaching) in the same meeting. For example, listed below are a number of comments made by the former president of Dynamic Controls/HS, Inc. at one of his staff meetings:

- "We need to reduce the number and length of our procedures and policies by 50 percent." (Challenge)
- "We have to do better, be quicker. What will it take?" (Challenge)

- "I believe we have the right people assembled to solve the overdue problem." (Confidence)

- "I trust that you will have your reports in by next Thursday." (Confidence)

- "The first step is to make all assumptions visible." (Coaching)

- "Part of understanding a process is knowing what customers do with the output." (Coaching)

Coaching, building confidence, and challenging the status quo are the building blocks of leadership. In the book *Jesus, CEO: Using Ancient Wisdom for Visionary Leadership*, author Laurie Beth Jones states that Jesus was a great leader and would have made a great CEO. He recruited twelve people who went on to dramatically influence the world. How did he do it? In my opinion, he followed precisely the **3-C Leadership Model**. What specific actions did he take?

1. He challenged people. He challenged his twelve recruits to give up their current jobs to take on a bigger and more meaningful task. He challenged people to think and act morally and ethically. He challenged people to always do what was right. Jesus knew that his role was to change the status quo.

2. He built confidence. He believed in his recruits. He saw great potential in each of them. When they failed, he didn't judge them— rather, he encouraged them to keep trying. Jesus gave them responsibility and authority to spread the word of God. Their accomplishments and successes were celebrated.

3. He coached. He believed his role was to help and nurture others. He called himself "the Shepherd." There are countless stories of Jesus teaching and preaching wherever he went. He trained his staff so effectively that they continued to do the work even after his death.

The signs of outstanding leadership often appear among the leader's followers. For example, are your followers

- challenging themselves to achieve stretch goals?

- confident in their abilities and decision-making skills?

- continuously learning new skills and strategies?

The following chapters describe additional ways you can challenge people, build their confidence, and coach them to greater levels of success.

At the end of each major section, one or more case studies will be presented that describe how various leaders have implemented the **3-C Leadership Model**. The first case studies highlight Sue Lewis and Bob La Palme. Sue is the executive vice president and chief real estate officer at The Travelers, and Bob is the chief financial officer at Jen-Coat, Inc.

Leaders redefine what's possible.

—sign above the desk of an executive at an automotive company

Case Study—Applying the 3-C Leadership Model

Each person and team is unique and has its own set of needs. There is no one leadership approach that fits all situations. Many leaders are good at only one or two of the Cs but not all three. In today's business world, challenge is common. What's often missing is coaching and building confidence to help people face the challenge.

Regarding challenge, I look for ways to push people out of their comfort zones, but not in a way that will paralyze them. Like throwing a rock in a pond, I try to stretch people one ripple at a time. When challenges are given, I provide people with a backdrop to put the goal in context. People want to know why their company cares about this particular goal and why they should care. I also find it helpful to describe what it will be like a year from now if we accomplish the objective. Once challenges are in place, I periodically check in with people to see what's happening. What obstacles are they facing? What's working and not working? This gives me insight in terms of what I need to do in the areas of confidence building and coaching. People need confidence to take risks. They also need to know what happens if they don't achieve the improvement target. A key lesson I've learned is that I need to set the example. No one will stretch more than I do. In addition, I have to demonstrate self-confidence to take risks and try radical approaches if necessary.

Leaders need to develop their own styles and approaches to each of the Cs. It's not enough just to challenge people. Accomplished business leaders are comfortable taking risks and performing at the top of their game. However, many people need coaching to develop the skills and mind-set to compete with the best. Effective leaders help people achieve their potential by engaging in all 3 Cs.

—Sue Lewis

Executive Vice President and
Chief Real Estate Officer
The Travelers

▲

Case Study—Applying the 3-C Leadership Model

I challenge people by giving them new tasks or projects that stretch their current skills and often require them to develop new skills. For example, we are currently implementing a corporate-wide People-Soft system. Several individuals have been given responsibility to implement specific modules. These asssignments are outside the people's normal job responsibilities. They are a challenge. Another way I challenge people in my department is by asking them to develop better ways to do their current jobs. It's important that all employees realize they must measure up to higher and higher performance standards.

Our company is going through tremendous growth. Other companies have gone through extensive downsizing. Both of these experiences can produce feelings of fear and insecurity. What people need is a clear understanding of their role in the ever-changing organization and an inner confidence to deal with today's constant rate of change. When people lack courage and confidence, they want to just keep doing what they've been doing. To build confidence I start by making sure people clearly understand the challenge they face. If people don't fully comprehend the challenge, they don't see the need to change or learn new skills. Making sure people have the appropriate training is also very important.

I often coach people one-on-one in my office. If people come to me with a problem, I require them to bring a solution. I don't want to own the problem. I coach people by asking questions. The right question helps people make decisions for themselves. I also think it's very important to constructively debate tough issues. At staff meetings I encourage dissenting points of view.

The 3 C Leadership Model is a useful tool. It's logical. Encourage people to stretch by giving them tough challenges. Build their confidence so they believe in themselves. Coach them in how to succeed. Leaders find ways to effectively perform each role.

—Bob La Palme

CFO
Jen-Coat, Inc.

PART II
Challenging the Status Quo

As individuals and groups pursue their goals, they may at times become complacent: "We're doing a fine job. We really can't make any additional improvements." Many change efforts and improvement programs fail because of complacency. If people see no need to change or improve results, then not much happens. Leaders are required to create and lead change, even when followers don't see the need. As one seminar participant stated, "Leaders must challenge the way things were done in the past. What was great last year may be just average this year."

Effective leaders challenge the comfort zone; they push people by setting world-class goals and standards of excellence. In his book *Leading Change,* Harvard Business School professor John P. Kotter contends that the biggest mistake many leaders make is that they don't establish a sense of urgency before trying to implement change. These leaders underestimate how hard it is to drive people out of their comfort zones. Dave, an employee from a manufacturing company, states, "Most of us are comfortable in the environments we have created. We identify with our sets of habits, attitudes, and activities." He goes on to say that people are often kept from changing because of loyalty to friends, family, self-image, or even a memory of the "good old days."

In a *Harvard Business Review* article entitled "The Work of Leadership," Ronald Heifetz and Donald Laurie make it clear what's expected of today's leader. They state that rather than provide all the answers, leaders have to ask tough questions. The right question forces people to rethink what they do and why they do it. Instead of maintaining the status quo, leaders have to challenge "the way we do business" and help others distinguish between core values

THE 3C LEADERSHIP MODEL

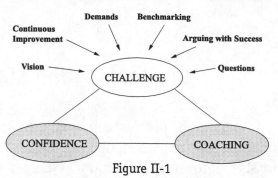

Figure II-1

and business practices that must change. Actress Cicely Tyson says that challenges make you discover aspects of yourself that you never knew existed. Challenges are what make you stretch and go beyond the norm.

The following pages list a number of additional ways leaders can challenge people to think and act in new ways. It's important that challenges be presented in such a way that they tie to business conditions and the marketplace. Followers want to know why they need to cut costs by 40 percent or improve cycle time from eight weeks to two days. If leaders don't clearly and convincingly explain why major improvements are needed, associates will not sign up for the effort.

The following are several approaches leaders can use to challenge followers (see figure II-1):

- State a Challenging Vision
- Demand the Impossible
- Ask Challenging Questions
- Create a Culture of Continuous Improvement
- Benchmark the Best
- Argue with Success

CHAPTER 2
State a Challenging Vision

The vision of PepsiCo is as follows: "To become the best consumer-products company in the world by consistently generating the highest return to shareholders." Many vision statements include the word "best," and to be the best at anything is certainly a challenge. Some visions provide a challenge by setting a quantitative goal, such as "achieving a 20 percent average annual return on stockholders' equity." Others make qualitative statements, such as "produce superior advertising" or "help them [people] attain the quality of life guaranteed in the American dream—sooner, better, and more conveniently than anyone else."

These visions challenge people to work at a higher level to achieve the desired goal. A vision expresses a desired future state that is better in some important way than what currently exists. It describes where you will be in the future and what it will be like. (See figure 2.1.) Visions are challenging in that they describe people and organizations not as they are but as they can become. A vision

VISION

It is said that a picture is worth a thousand words. What pictures do you create for your followers?

- Is your picture clear?
- What is different from today?
- What challenges are implied?
- What skills and talents will people need?

Figure 2.1

starts with what the leader really cares about and is fully committed to achieving. Dreams and visions can be the driving force that moves individuals, teams, and companies to work at a higher level and achieve great performance. In *The Leadership Challenge*, authors James Kouzes and Barry Posner make the point that in some ways, leaders live their lives backward. They have a vision or picture in their mind's eye of what the result looks like. They then work backward and figure out what steps need to be taken to achieve this vision.

What are the features of a challenging vision? It is simple and straightforward and describes a level of excellence required in the future. One executive states, "Aim high. People will not work hard and long to achieve insignificant results. Trying to become the 'best' at something is what gets the adrenaline pumping." One of my colleagues states, "Companies need to be good in many areas but they should strive to be the best in at least one thing. Visions need to stake out the area where they will be number one."

Without a vision it's business as usual. People keep doing what they have done in the past. Effective leaders, like evangelists, constantly preach and sell their visions. They help people picture what it will be like if they reach their goals and what will happen if they don't. By showing why the status quo is unacceptable, leaders create discomfort about existing attitudes and behavior and thus lay the foundation for change. For example, business leaders such as Jack Welch, Roger Milliken, Anita Roderick, Lou Gerstner, and Charlotte Beers have compelling visions for their corporations. Their visions have challenged people to achieve far beyond what others thought was possible. Great visions often precede great accomplishments.

Here are some points to keep in mind when creating a vision:

1. Steps to Creating a Challenging Vision. A vision is a picture of the future. It is the result of looking beyond *what is* to *what could be*. Creating a vision doesn't happen overnight. It requires a lot of time, effort, and discussion about the future.

What are the steps? Recommendations from the experts include

- visiting top companies,

- holding discussions with key customers and suppliers,

- identifying technology trends,

- analyzing trends in other industries, and

- identifying current and future business challenges.

From these inputs the leader must create a picture of the future. In what ways will the future be different and better? Leaders must also look within themselves to focus on what they value. What gets them excited? What they are willing to risk?

2. Components of a Vision. An effective vision appeals to people's intellect and emotions. The vision tells people not only what the future can be like but also how it will feel. Remember the times when you said with passion and enthusiasm, "It's a boy!" "We won the game!" "I love you!" The people you were speaking to became interested and excited. In a similar way, a vision excites people. A vision serves to inspire; it's a reminder of why you keep going when you would rather quit. It adds meaning and motivation. An executive in one of my seminars stated, "A vision acts like a magnet pulling people's focus and energy to the challenge of a better future."

3. Organization/Selling of a Vision. Try organizing your vision into several formats, such as a twenty-word summary, a picture, a metaphor, a slogan, and a television commercial. Look for the salient images and phrases that best capture your view of the future. What are the features and benefits of your vision? Features are the characteristics of the vision, such as what it will look like and feel like and how organization will operate. Benefits, on the other hand, answer the question, So what? The benefits of a vision describe how it will help people, how conditions will be better.

When major change is occurring, it's natural for people to focus on what they are giving up. Leaders need to help people focus on what's to be gained. Leaders must also remember there is always a group of people who resist change and hold on to the status quo. Selling one's vision often involves overcoming objections from people who like conditions just the way they are.

Communicating Your Vision

Management consultants Thomas Werner and Robert Lynch recommend that anytime a leader is making a significant change, he or she should follow the 7 x 7 communication rule. (See figure 2.2.) In essence, the 7 x 7 communication rule requires you to communicate the message (your vision) seven times using seven different techniques. In my experience effective leaders are passionate about their visions and discuss them at every opportunity. Using multiple communication approaches helps ensure the messages are heard and understood. One general manager states, "I not only use a variety of approaches to communicate my vision, but I also start every staff meeting with an overhead slide that describes our vision and key strategies. It's a constant reminder of where we're going and how we're going to get there."

Another communication technique frequently used by leaders is storytelling. Why are stories such powerful verbal tools? Stories are engaging. People relate to the information both intellectually

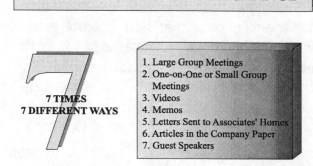

COMMUNICATING MAJOR CHANGE

7 TIMES
7 DIFFERENT WAYS

1. Large Group Meetings
2. One-on-One or Small Group
   Meetings
3. Videos
4. Memos
5. Letters Sent to Associates' Homes
6. Articles in the Company Paper
7. Guest Speakers

Figure 2.2

and emotionally. Stories provide messages that people can interpret and relate to from their own perspectives. Leaders' stories usually have these elements:

- A case for change (the challenge)
- Obstacles to confront
- An expressed belief in people (building confidence)
- Lessons or morals (coaching)

The classic business story is much like the classic human story. It involves a challenge, the overcoming of great odds, the courage and confidence needed to deal with the situation, the upholding of values and principles, and the lessons learned for the future. Effective stories can make a leader's vision come alive. They also can illustrate in a very powerful way what it takes to reach the top of the hill.

Conclusion—State a Challenging Vision

Karl J. Krapek, former president of Pratt & Whitney Aircraft, a division of United Technologies, Inc., said the following to his workforce:

> Imagine what it would be like starting a new century working for the undisputed industry leader.
>
> Picture us as sole-source engine supplier for the Boeing 747-500 and -600 as those new models enter service at the turn of the century; our PW600 as the exclusive powerplant for the Asian Express, with 300 orders from Chinese airlines alone; and our PK6 engine powering a new generation of Russian-built helicopters, regional and utility aircraft.
>
> We can make Pratt & Whitney world-class, with more reliable products, better service, greater productivity, and stronger financial returns than G.E.

His vision challenged the status quo. He challenged people to consider being the industry leader, being the best. Krapek went on to discuss how this vision of the future could be realized. The "how to do it" comments also focused on the company's values, which include the following:

To stand in the shoes of our customer.

To know that our customers see us through the eyes of employees.

To share information in an honest, complete, and timely way.

To continuously benchmark our products and processes against the best in the industry.

To question our most basic assumptions and improve our most accepted practices.

To make decisions that add to shareholder value.

To create an environment that values employees from diverse cultural, educational, and professional backgrounds.

Winning leaders are never satisfied with the status quo. They are always challenging people to rise to a new level of performance. A challenging vision helps people clearly see a better, more exciting future. It energizes people to leave the comfort of the present to pursue a more rewarding and satisfying future.

Be Passionate about That Which You Do— With Enough Passion, the Fullest Potential Will Be Reached.

—sign on the office wall of Judi Missett, President, Jazzercise, Inc.

CHAPTER 3
Demand The Impossible

Jack Welch, CEO of General Electric, has a philosophy of setting "stretch goals." Lawrence Bossidy, CEO of AlliedSignal, requires his managers to establish "killer goals." William Hewlett, of Hewlett Packard, states, "Improve performance by 50 percent." George David, CEO of United Technologies, says that leaders need to set standards higher and higher—higher than anyone thinks realistically can be set.

These leaders challenge others by setting goals that are significantly outside people's comfort zones. How do people react to these types of impossible goals? With comments such as "You can't be serious" and "There's no way we can double productivity." Leaders who establish stretch or killer goals are striving for huge gains in performance while having no idea how to attain them. However, these leaders also have great confidence that their people will figure out ways to achieve these step-change improvements. The fundamental belief is that the potential for major increases in performance exists in everyone. In general, top leaders believe that most people possess far more energy, talent, and ability than they realize.

Killer goals can't be accomplished by simply working harder. Dennis Gormley, CEO at Federal-Mogul Corporation, says that an impossible goal forces you to rethink everything. It forces you to break away from all the old habits and traditions. Starting with a clean sheet of paper and utilizing creative thinking techniques are mandatory. In a November 1995 *Fortune* magazine article by Strat S. Sherman, Steve Kern, chief learning officer at GE, states that leaders who set stretch goals are trying to get people to think of fundamentally better ways of performing their work. The motto needs to be "Don't try harder, try different." A killer goal forces individuals and teams to do their very best creative thinking to formulate breakthrough ideas. A participant in one of my leadership seminars stated, "Challenging assumptions is critical. Throw the rule book away. If you don't challenge assumptions, your creativity is limited by custom and convention."

In the article, Kern goes on to say that if you set stretch goals, don't punish failure. Let's be realistic—individuals and teams aren't going to achieve every stretch goal. It's important for leaders to recognize the effort and hard work that go into trying to achieve a goal even if results fall short of the target. Bill Harris, executive vice president of Intuit, says that rewarding success is easy but rewarding intelligent failure is more important. Don't judge people strictly by results; also consider the quality of their efforts.

Why don't managers and leaders demand more? I believe there are several reasons:

1. Many managers and leaders want to be liked. They don't set "impossible" goals because they know people react with anger and resentment toward the person setting the goals.

2. Some managers have a fear of failure: "What if I set these tough targets and then we don't hit them?"

3. Some managers believe that people's workload is already heavy, and stretch goals will put them over the edge. People will be demotivated and they will do less work, not more.

I believe there is an inverse relationship between people's leadership potential and their need to be liked. People who have a great need to be liked will not take the aggressive steps needed to challenge people to leave their comfort zones. They "set the bar" low so everyone can jump over. (See figure 3.1.)

Certainly, some people will react negatively to stretch goals, but others will step up to the challenge, especially when they clearly understand the business drivers. An executive stated, "When people

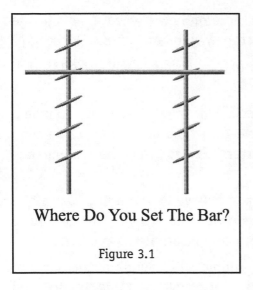

Where Do You Set The Bar?

Figure 3.1

are put to the test, it's amazing what some can do and will do to get the job done." In a 1991 *Harvard Business Review* article, Robert H. Schaffer makes this same point when he describes how two Motorola employees recounted their experience on a project to produce a product for Nippon Telephone and Telegraph. The employees said that the customer wanted nothing except absolute excellence. Their team was excited by the challenge of doing a task that was considered impossible. They were highly motivated to succeed in this program. They said that this assignment was the most exciting project they had ever been assigned.

In my own research I have asked people this question: "Think about the toughest work challenge you've had in the last three years. How did you feel when you were initially given the assignment?" Responses have included the following:

- Excited, challenged, nervous, and motivated to do a great job.

- Overwhelmed, intimidated, challenged, excited.

- Enthusiastic about being able to make a significant contribution.

- Excited but hesitant.

- Important.

A tough challenge that significantly impacts a company's performance can be intimidating, but it also excites people.

To create this type of environment, leaders must worry less about people liking them and focus more on how to create a challenge culture that helps people reach new standards of excellence.

Here are some additional points to consider when setting stretch goals:

- Establish goals that are specific, measurable, and time bounded. "I want you to reduce cycle time from 42 days to 12 days by the end of the third quarter." Explain why the step-change improvement is needed.

- Make it clear you expect and believe the stretch goals will be achieved. "I'm confident you will find a way to get it done. I believe you have the talents and creativity to succeed."

- Expect resistance. Some people will complain and say the goals are totally unrealistic. Let people vent but stay focused on the target.

- Empower people. "You have the authority to assign tasks and manage the budget." Let people figure out how to achieve the goal.

- Celebrate success. Short-term wins are important. "We've completed phase one, a team celebration is scheduled for Friday."

Conclusion—Demand the Impossible

Sometimes institutions such as colleges and universities "demand the impossible." The Sloan Fellows Program at the Massachusetts Institute of Technology (MIT) is considered to be one of the best and toughest graduate management programs in the country. One of my colleagues, Vin Misciagna, attended the program several years ago. He states, "The Sloan Fellows Program is designed to stress an individual through the assignment of large amounts of homework in areas such as finance, accounting, human resources, and organizational research. An average homework assignment would require five to seven hours of work each night. In addition, there were longer term projects, including a research paper and thesis, required for graduation."

He goes on to say the pressure required him to be creative. He had to take steps above and beyond what he considered normal in any previous educational experience. The Sloan program requires students to stretch farther than they think they can. Vin states, "The sacrifice and hard work were worth the investment because of the prestige associated with obtaining a graduate degree from MIT's Sloan school." When leaders establish "stretch" or "killer" goals, people are challenged to dig deep and find the motivation to meet the heightened expectations. People can and do rise to the occasion when they are given a tough, demanding challenge.

Separate What Needs to Be Done
from How Difficult It Is to Get It Done.

—sign on the desk of a middle manager at a large manufacturing company

CHAPTER 4
Ask Challenging Questions

Asking questions is another way to challenge current methods of operation. David Glass, CEO of Wal-Mart, thrives on asking hundreds of questions. His questions challenge his senior executives to listen, learn, and change. Leadership often involves asking the right questions at the right time. I have heard leaders ask questions that challenge people to think differently, to question what worked in the past, and to question why situations can't be changed. A participant in one of my leadership seminars put it this way: "The quality of our work as leaders depends significantly on the questions we ask. A simple but provocative question is often the first step in any change initiative." (See figure 4.1.)

LEADERSHIP QUESTIONS

What question will help people face reality?

What question will energize people?

What new question needs to be asked?

Figure 4.1

Why? is a penetrating question. It forces people to look at the tacit rules and assumptions that underlie the way business is conducted. Asking Why? forces people to evaluate whether the current assumptions are still valid. Bruce Gissing, executive vice president of Boeing Aircraft Company, said, "World-class managers are genuinely curious. In a search for hidden problems, their favorite question is 'Why?'" For example, "Why do we follow that procedure?" "Why do we make that assumption?" "Why do we do the work here?"

An executive at Kodak says, "If someone says it takes six months to do something, I say, 'Why can't we do it in a month?'" Imagine the benefits of constantly, incessantly questioning every report, rule, policy, system process, and procedure with a simple question: "Why are we doing this?"

In problem-solving situations, experts recommend asking Why? at least five times. Practicing this approach helps you break through the symptoms and identify the root cause of a problem. Another good question to ask is What if? The inventor of Nike Shoes asked, "What happens if I pour rubber into my waffle iron?" That simple "what if" question revolutionized the athletic shoe industry. Leaders can challenge current thinking and behavior by asking, "What if we tried X?" "What if" questions penetrate the comfort zone and plant seeds for people to consider new ideas and new possibilities.

A CEO of a major corporation is fond of saying, "Better questions produce better results." Leaders need to consider, "What's the right question for the current situation?" "What question will get people to think or act differently?" Michael Jones, author of *Creating an Imaginative Life*, says that questions generate energy and focus energy in the direction needed to answer the questions.

Some of my colleagues have made the point that in many companies, asking questions is viewed as an admission of ignorance. In their meetings, few, if any, questions are asked. Asking questions needs to be encouraged and viewed as a desire to learn and gain understanding. Effective leaders ask numerous questions and encourage others to do the same. Here are several examples of thought-provoking and challenging questions.

- "What today is impossible to do but would fundamentally change your business?" —*Joel Barker*
- "What great thing in life would you attempt if you knew it was impossible to fail?" —*Dr. Robert Schuller*

- "Do you want to work for a mediocre company or a great one?" —*Larry Bossidy, CEO, AlliedSignal*

- "Every project we take starts with a question: How can we do what's never been done before?" —*Stuart Hornery, retired chairman, Lend Lease Corporation*

- What is impossible to do today but would fundamentally change your customers' business?

- How does the customer define excellence?

- What's the industry's best practice for cycle time? cost? quality? cash flow? inventory turns?

The right question opens people's minds to ponder and consider new possibilities. "How can we do what's never been done before?" Great question. Leaders know that powerful ideas create change. Ideas flow from questions. Questions are the stimulus. New ideas and new relationships are the responses.

Business and individual change often occurs when new answers are found to simple questions. I've watched and helped several senior management teams deal with three simple questions.

- What's our mission/purpose?

- What's our vision?

- What are our key values?

As new answers evolved to each question, it was exciting, liberating, and transforming.

Conclusion—Ask Challenging Questions

A former secretary of state of the United States gave an assignment to one of his aides to write a position paper on a sensitive Middle East problem. After several weeks of research and writing, the aide presented his report. The secretary of state asked,

"Is this your best work?" The aide said, "Well, I probably could do better. Let me take it back and do some additional work on it." A few days later the aide turned in the revised report. The next day the secretary of state met with the aide and said, "Is this your best work?" The aide said, "Well, maybe I can do better." This cycle repeated one more time. Finally, the aide presented the report and said, "This is my best work." The secretary of state said, "Fine, now I will read it."

The repeated question, "Is this your best work?" challenged the aide to do his best work. The best leaders frequently ask questions that challenge people to raise their performance level. Of course, leaders not only ask great questions but also drive for answers that meet the requirements of best-in-class performance.

The Manager Asks: Who, What, When, and Where.
The Leader Asks <u>Why</u> and Keeps Asking Why Until All
Assumptions and Beliefs Are Revealed.

—sign on the office wall of Dan Kelly, Vice President, Transportation Business,
International Fuel Cells

CHAPTER 5
Create a Culture of Continuous Improvement

Some companies create a work culture that constantly challenges all employees to improve their performance. Allen Sheppard, CEO of Grand Met, has installed what he calls "the Challenge Culture." He pushes himself and others to the limits of their performance and urges them to do better. The company culture can be summarized as "Don't think best, think better. How can it be done better next time?" Woody Morcatt, chairman and CEO of Dana Corporation, challenges each of his employees to submit two new ideas every month that can be implemented in the individual's work area. The goal is to implement 80 percent of these improvement ideas. Such a challenge inspires employees, strikes a fatal blow to complacency, and encourages continuous improvement.

Osana Lida, executive vice president of Honda North America, described the company's "challenging spirit" with these words:

> Throughout our history, most of Honda's great achievements have been the result of accepting new challenges that focus and motivate everyone in the company. Challenges that are sometimes self-imposed. Or challenges from the competitive marketplace. Or challenges that ensue from government regulation.

Some leaders create a "challenge culture" by putting up motivational posters and office wall quotes, such as the following:

- "Past Good Performance Won't Make It in the Future"
- "Best Is the Enemy of Better"
- "Good Enough Isn't Good Enough; Better Is What Counts"

These messages help create a work environment where constant improvement is the norm. In such an environment, no employee has the attitude "If it ain't broke, don't fix it." Rather, everyone is striving to improve his or her process every day.

Continuous improvement is not a one-time event, it's ongoing. To make this point, an operations director begins his weekly staff meetings this way: "Okay, folks, tell me what records you broke this week. If you didn't break records, you didn't improve." That challenge sends a clear message and keeps people energized and focused on improving results. I believe most people have gotten the "improvement message" and have taken steps to improve their processes once or twice. The real task, though, is rising to the "change and improve" challenge again and again. People who keep learning and finding better ways week after week are the ones who achieve ongoing success. (See figure 5.1.)

LEADERS WITH A CONTINUOUS-IMPROVEMENT MIND-SET

- Strong desire to improve
- Commitment to candid self-assessment
- Strong curiosity
- Ability to learn from both success and failure
- Nondefensive response to negative feedback
- Willingness to experiment and try new approaches

Figure 5.1

Companies that have the motto "Business as usual" are filing for Chapter 11 bankruptcy. Michael Sinjard of Specialized, Inc., inventor of the mountain bike, teaches his employees the slogan

"Innovate or die!" Innovation almost always grows out of trial-and-error learning. The more attempts you make, the quicker you gain insight and the faster you discover breakthrough ideas. Robert Meers, president of Reebok Brands, one of the leading makers of athletic footwear, said that for Reebok to become a better company it had to take on the challenge of reinventing itself again and again and yet again. In a similar way, Meers indicates that he has had to continuously reinvent himself over the past 30 years. He went from being a football player at the University of Massachusetts with goals of playing professional football to a businessman, to an entrepreneur, to a corporate manager, to his current position of running a $3.5 billion corporation. He plans soon to reinvent himself one more time.

Culture is defined as the ways of thinking and behaving that members of an organization have in common. Typically, that includes shared values, beliefs, and behavior expectations. Leaders shape their company's culture by what they say and do. Specifically, stories, rituals, ceremonies, and what's identified as "high priority" all send important messages about the culture. One executive states, "We have a culture of mediocrity. Meetings begin late. There is a general acceptance of missed deadlines and the avoidance of risks." Leaders also impact the culture by their reaction to poor performance such as missed deadlines. To what extent are people held accountable? The best leaders set the example by continuously improving their own performance as well as holding other people accountable for improved resuls.

In one of my leadership seminars, I asked participants to describe the leaders who had exemplified an attitude of continuous improvement at their companies. Comments included:

- He had high expectations of himself and his group. Improvement was expected.

- ... very curious and always benchmarking. Always trying to learn from best practices.

- Ray was fond of asking these questions: What are you measuring? Why? What's the trend line look like?

- She made us all learn and use the TQM (Total Quality Management) tools to improve our process.

- Jim made us learn from our mistakes. Lessons-learned meetings were mandatory.

- There was lots of encouragement to improve the hard numbers. She also stressed that continuous improvement of our attitude, motivation, and interpersonal skills was needed.

In essence, leaders create a continuous improvement culture by what they say and do. Leaders start by setting the example; they measure results, hold people accountable, and celebrate success.

Conclusion—Create a Culture of Continuous Improvement

To create a culture of continuous improvement, one medium-sized company (750 employees) established a specific weekly meeting dedicated to process improvements. This meeting is in addition to a weekly "staff" meeting that focuses on running the day-to-day business. The group that meets at the separate meeting is called the Quality Council. The Council is made up of the president, his direct reports, four associate members, and a designated Continuous Improvement Advocate (CIA).

These meetings focus on the vital few critical processes required to achieve the company's strategic goals. Quality tools such as flowcharts, scatter diagrams, pareto analysis, and fishbone diagrams are used to understand current processes as well as development improvement recommendations. In addition, teams are often chartered to research specific problems. Chartered teams report their recommendations and identify barriers to implementation. A Council member states, "Spending time on process improvements sends a strong message to the organization. People know continuous improvement is expected. It's not an optional task; it's required for our survival." When the senior management team commits its time and energy to continuous improvement, the organization responds in a like manner. Everyone in this organization is challenged to "find a better way."

Good enough isn't good enough. Better is what counts. Doing it <u>better</u> requires desire, determination, curiosity, benchmarking, experimentation, and constant learning.

—sign on the office wall of a quality manager at a large aerospace company

CHAPTER 6
Benchmark the Best

Benchmarking is another way leaders can challenge people to improve their operations. Benchmarking is a process of measuring or comparing your process against the best in the world. (See figure 6.1.) It includes observing and studying what top companies do to achieve outstanding results. Sam Walton, the founder of Wal-Mart, said that he spent more time in his competitors' stores than they themselves did. He readily admitted that many of his best ideas came from observing what other stores were doing.

BENCHMARKING

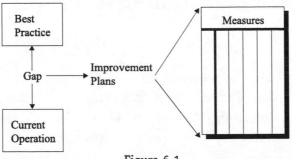

Figure 6.1

Organizational psychologist Carla O'Nell, Ph.D., says that without an external example, the goals for improvement are likely to be "the same as last year, plus 5 percent." That often won't be enough in today's competitive marketplace. External evidence of what other companies are achieving makes stretch goals, such as a 30 percent cost reduction, very real and believable. Benchmarking also provides specific metrics, which adds validity to the position that major improvements are possible.

Visiting top-performing companies can have a dramatic impact. One executive states, "Nothing convinces someone faster than seeing a world-class operation. Observing a factory or company that produces three times as much as you do makes a lasting impression." Benchmarking also gets the competitive juices flowing: "If they can produce fifty widgets an hour, we can make sixty." However, some people react with denial: "They're not in the same industry as we are." "I don't believe they're giving us the whole story." "They can't be that good." Sometimes, further discussion or a second trip to the company is necessary to break through the denial.

Benchmarking not only shows people what's possible but also gives them a chance to see *how* business is done. One of the coaching techniques I describe is "Show People What Good Performance Looks Like" (chapter 15). An excellent first step in any coaching situation is providing a concrete example of how to do a task. Site visits to top-performing companies provide an opportunity to see specifically what people do to achieve their outstanding results.

To take advantage of benchmarking's benefits, start by following these tips:

1. Understand the way you already do business. Linda Crosby DeBerry of Federal Express states that many benchmarking attempts fail because companies don't know their own processes, so they don't know what they're looking for elsewhere.

2. Determine which organizations excel at the target process. Ask suppliers and customers for their opinions. Research the literature. Industry associations are also a good source for identifying potential organizations to benchmark.

3. Develop good questions. Be ready to ask specifically for what you want to know. Here are some suggestions from Rob Porro, consultant and trainer, who teaches a seminar on benchmarking:

- Ask people who do similar work in your organization to help create relevant questions.

- Begin with easy questions and work up to more difficult ones.

- Develop follow-up questions as necessary.

- Determine your own unit's answer to each quesion.

4. Contact the human resources or public relations department of the organization you wish to benchmark, explain your purpose, and ask for a referral. Establish a mutually convenient date and time to visit the company or conduct a telephone interview. (If the organization isn't interested in participating, don't press. Benchmarking won't work unless both parties are happy to participate.)

5. Make the most of the site visit. Introduce everyone who participates and explain why they're there. Provide and adhere to an agenda.

After the site visit, assemble your team and discuss what you learned. What are the performance gaps between your current practices and the best practices? What new targets or goals can be established? What best practices can be implemented?

In their book, *The Leadership Engine,* authors Noel Tichy and Eli Cohen make the point that winning leaders make stretch goals seem attainable by building up people's confidence and determination. They acknowledge the difficulty of exceeding benchmark targets and creating a teamwork attitude; however, they say, "If we work together as a team, we can succeed." Most experts believe it is best to focus on one or two important changes that can be achieved within three months. By focusing on visible short-term results, you build momentum, credibility, and confidence in people's ability to change.

Sometimes, benchmarking can provide a boost of confidence. If you benchmark the best companies and find that your process performance is comparable, this discovery can be a strong vote of confidence that you will succeed. However, you can't become complacent. Remember, the competition isn't settling for the status quo. Chances are that they are also out benchmarking the very best practices to improve their process and product.

Conclusion—Benchmark the Best

A large manufacturing company with multiple plants had experienced an injury rate of seven injuries per one hundred employees. Typically, one of these injuries resulted in an employee being out of work for an average of twenty days. These metrics had improved from five years ago but hadn't changed much in the past two years. About this time Chris Wiernicki was hired as manager of the company's safety program. Chris's vision statement to senior management was "Let's eliminate all accidents and injuries." Certainly that's a worthy goal; however, few people believed it was doable. Benchmarking found that the best-in- class companies did have significantly fewer injuries. The best companies had between .3 and .8 injuries for every hundred employees. In this situation, benchmarking proved a step-change improvement was possible. Chris states, "Benchmarking challenged management's thinking. No one believed a goal of zero injuries was possible. Benchmarking showed that other companies were already operating close to the no-injuries rate."

Chris's next step was to study the current quality systems, policies, procedures, and training used at the company. Some policies and procedures needed to be rewritten and simplified. However, those changes alone weren't going to achieve the goal of zero injuries. New research indicated that 90 percent of accidents in the workplace result from unsafe acts by people, not unsafe conditions. Chris concluded that to achieve zero accidents and injuries, a new culture regarding safety was needed. Over the next eighteen months, both hourly and salaried employees attended seminars and workshops aimed at getting people to examine their assumptions, beliefs, and attitudes toward safety. As a new safety culture took hold, injuries dropped significantly.

Leaders like Chris aren't satisfied with the status quo. They believe a better future is possible. Benchmarking best practices provides concrete examples of how others have found a way to make significant improvements.

Benchmarking

The Practice: Find the best, then improve it.
The Psychology: Being open to change/undo
what you previously created.

—written on a flipchart in a training room at the Heritage Conference
Center, Southbury, CT

CHAPTER 7
Argue with Success

Pay attention to what leaders have to say about success:

- Successful companies tend to get complacent. They don't really know until it's too late that the marketplace has changed.

- Success is seductive. It creates the comforting illusion that if you keep doing what you've been doing, you'll keep on being successful.

- Success makes the status quo become the measure of success, and the entire organization becomes more bureaucratic and less entrepreneurial. The organization becomes more difficult to change.

After achieving success, many individuals and business leaders lose their motivation. They develop the attitude "Why change? I've been successful." Success creates a false sense of security: "If I keep doing what I've been doing, I'll continue to be a success." The more successful a company is, the more inward focused it becomes. The truth is that success often leads to failure because people lose their hunger to improve and beat the competition. Bill Gates has an autographed picture of Henry Ford above his desk. It's a reminder not to become complacent. Henry Ford let himself and his company become complacent and lose market share. Ford eventually ceded industry leadership to Alfred Sloan, chairman of General Motors.

In the November–December 1995 issue of *Business Horizons*, Jack Miller, president and founder of Quill Corporation, made the point that the adage "Don't argue with success" is wrong. Miller states that when you don't argue, constantly and unremittingly, with your own success, you're doomed to eventual failure. Many companies, including the big ones such as Sears, General Motors, and AT&T, literally have had to "reinvent" themselves to remain viable. Permanent success is guaranteed to no one. Of the top one hundred firms on the first Fortune list in 1956, only twenty-seven were still ranked there by 1989. The president of a small company stated, "The day the management of any company thinks it has succeeded and has finished its process of reinvention is the day the company starts sliding backward. Successful leaders keep updating their ideas and business strategies to keep them appropriate in an ever-changing marketplace."

Leaders need to make a habit of "arguing with success." But how do you get people to argue with their own success? What can leaders do? It really comes down to challenging people's thinking and making sure they have the right attitude to fight complacency. Here are some approaches to consider:

1. Not all customers are happy. Bring in the unhappy customers and let them speak directly to employees about what service and product improvements are needed.

2. Point out other companies (benchmarking) that are making significant improvements in their operations. "If they have cut cost or cycle time by 30 percent, why can't we?"

3. Demand more. If your son or daughter came home with all Bs on a report card, would you challenge him or her to get three As on the next report card? Demanding higher performance can fight the tendency to become complacent.

4. Avoid happy talk and generalizations. When people start making statements such as "We had a great year," "Isn't it wonderful that ...?" "We hit a home run," or "We have a few problems, but they're no big deal," stop them and get specific. Last year's performance may have been great, but chances are that some problems occurred and performance in some areas needs improvement. You may have won the game, but how many errors occurred? Also, it's always worth noting that this is a new year with new and tougher challenges. The competition is improving.

5. Focus on change. How is the marketplace changing? New technology? New regulations? New competition? New products? What impact do these changes have on the way we do business? What changes do we need to make in our business strategies?

Miller admits it's tough to constantly argue with success. He suggests the right attitude after achieving success is "I'm happy but not satisfied." Great leaders are always looking for a better way. They are never content with the status quo. (See figure 7.1.)

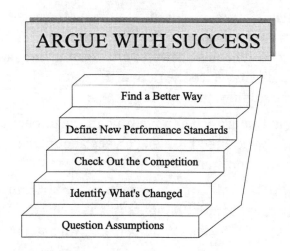

Figure 7.1

Conclusion—Argue with Success

My colleague, John Nicoletta, worked as an account executive for a recruiting/placement company that had twenty offices along the East Coast. Year after year his office was the most successful in terms of revenue generated as a result of placing people in positions such as accountant, financial analyst, and sales representative. What made his office so successful? John states, "The manager of our office challenged us constantly. He never let us get complacent. Every week you had to prove yourself."

The manager used the following techniques to "argue with success" and achieve better results every year:

1. Morning Meetings. Every day there was a meeting from 7:30 to 8:30 a.m. Part of the meeting was dedicated to teaching and training. The manager constantly brought in new information to help his staff improve their interviewing and placement skills. The second part of the meeting was a review of successes and failures from the previous day. The manager constantly asked questions such as "How did you make it happen?" "What new technique did you try?" "What can we learn from this situation?" "How would you do it next time?" John said, "We were constantly improving our skills and techniques on how to find and place good candidates."

2. Metrics. Daily, weekly, monthly, and quarterly metrics were kept on activities such as telephone contacts, job orders, interviews, and placements. These metrics were visible for all to see. Each account executive received frequent feedback and coaching on how to improve. John states, "You always knew exactly where you stood compared to the metrics." At the end of a quarter, the metrics board was wiped clean except for the year-to-date placements. It was as though each quarter, everybody went back to the starting line and had to prove himself or herself over the next three months. The culture was "What have you done for me lately?"

3. Objectives. Challenging objectives were set for everyone. Each account executive strived to be at or above the group average for revenue generated in the previous quarter. For example, if the average revenue produced in the first quarter was $100,000 per executive, then the objective for the second quarter was to produce $120,000 or more. Each quarter the challenge was bigger.

4. Challenged Success. John states, "Even when we were having a great quarter, our manager challenged us to think about new and different approaches."

Businesspeople have talked about how change is constant and unrelenting. I think a lot of people are secretly hoping that the waves of change initiatives will stop. People want to get back to "business as usual," back to the "comfort zone." That hasn't happened. With each passing year, it is increasingly clear that change is a fundamental part of doing business.

If you don't argue with success, you may find yourself being very unsuccessful.

—Elizabeth Thornton

SUMMARY
Challenging the Status Quo

Below is a list of leaders who stepped forward and challenged the status quo. They used different approaches, but their aim was to help people to think and act differently. Their challenges forced people to rethink their attitudes, behavior, and commitment.

Dr. Martin Luther King, Jr., challenged people by his vision/dream of a better world. In his August 28, 1963, "I Have a Dream" speech, he described a future of true equality, justice, freedom, opportunity, and brotherhood for all.

Bill Gates, CEO of Microsoft, challenged his organization to achieve the company's mission statement, "A computer on every desk and in every home."

President John F. Kennedy challenged people by stating "Ask not what your country can do for you but, rather, ask what you can do for your country." He also challenged the nation to land a man on the moon and return him safely to Earth by the end of the decade.

Betsy Barnard, president and CEO of Pacific Bell Communications, constantly challenges herself to leave her "comfort zone." She defines living outside her comfort zone as taking on bigger and greater responsibilities. It also means nonstop development of knowledge and skills and a willingness to step "outside the lines."

Pat Riley, NBA coach, challenges his players by using a Career Best Effort System, explained in his book, *The Winner Within*. First, all the players are tracked against their personal best performance, and they are compared with the best players who play similar positions on opposing teams.

Joel Barker, futurist, has challenged businesspeople by asking them to think about and answer this question: "What is impossible to do today but would fundamentally change your business?"

Carol Barty, CEO of design-software manufacturer Autodesk, refocused the company from a one-product design-automation-software company to one that has a core compentency of software design that can be applied in many markets. She challenged her organization to think of new and different applications for its software.

Alfred P. Sloan, chairman of General Motors from 1923 to 1946, challenged his staff to disagree, debate, and discuss issues before making a decision. When there was complete agreement on a decision, he would state, "I propose we postpone further discussion on this matter to give ourselves time to develop disagreement and gain understanding of what this decision is all about."

George David, president and CEO of United Technologies, Inc., challenged his employees to become the best-educated workforce on the planet. He backed up his challenge by providing a very generous educational assistance benefit.

Bob Galvin, chairman of the executive committee at Motorola, challenged his employees to achieve six sigma quality, which is 3.4 defects per million parts.

Thomas Edison, perhaps the most prolific inventor of all time, created a work environment of continuous experimentation leading to continuous improvement. On his desk he had a sign: "There's a way to do it better—find it."

All of these leaders challenged people to pursue higher goals and achieve more than they thought was possible. They used different approaches, but their goal was the same—to change the status quo, to create a better future.

We must reverse a paradigm drummed into us from business school to the grave: what worked in the past will work in the future.

—Dr. Gary Hamel

Case Studies—Applying the 3-C Leadership Model

Chapters 2–7 described numerous ways that leaders challenge people. In addition to challenging people, leaders build people's confidence and provide coaching on ways to be more effective and efficient. The following case studies describe how Ayn La Plant and Janice Deskus apply the **3-C Leadership Model**. Ayn is president of the Beekley Corporation, and Janice is the former director of human resources for Veeder-Root, a division of Danaher Corporation.

Case Study—Applying the 3-C Leadership Model

I find people love to be challenged. We challenge people in a number of ways. A key part of our culture is ARC, which stands for "Attitude, Results, and Continuous Improvement." Our culture demands ongoing improvement in each area. We challenge people to spend 15 to 20 percent of their worktime on learning and development activities. Beekley provides a variety of seminars and workshops as well as a library of books and videotapes. A key part of my job is people development, and that starts with challenging people to do better than they think they can.

Another way I challenge people is through a technique called "thought transmission." I ask questions that force people to find their own answers. The right question can also help people see an issue from a different angle. Asking questions that prod people to think differently can open up many new possibilities.

Benchmarking is another way we challenge people. I want our employees to look at other companies and find best practices. If you're really committed to continuous improvement, you have a natural curiosity to learn from the best.

On an operational level, all of our teams have five key goals that challenge and stretch them to be the industry leader. Establishing challenging goals is very important, but I've also learned I need to set the example. One of our initiatives is LBE—Lead by Example. I have to challenge myself. I constantly read books and articles, attend seminars, and network with other business leaders. I've also brought in several consultants who challenged us to rethink some of our strategies. If I don't practice continuous improvement, how can I expect others to continuously improve?

It's true people need confidence to handle today's demands and pressures. I fundamentally believe people can do whatever they set their minds to do. People are capable of unlimited development. In every meeting I try to convey my confidence in people. It may take the form of asking their opinion and showing I value their ideas. It may be verbally telling them "I know you will succeed," or it may be giving them candid feedback. I try to give feedback in such a way that the people know I believe in them.

Coaching and teaching are an important part of my job. I teach several components of our management and leadership seminars. This gives me a chance to formally present my ideas. Informally, I coach by helping people apply what they learn in the classroom or textbook. I also tell lots of stories. Good stories describe a specific situation that can be a springboard to discuss what was done and what other approaches might have been as effective, if not more effective. I want people to look for the "third right answer." There's more than one right answer.

Another part of coaching is giving feedback. One of our company initiatives is called "care to confront." It's kind of a tough love approach. People need to confront problems, face reality. If you don't deal with problems, they keep showing up. We use role playing to teach employees how to effectively confront problems.

The 3 Cs—challenge, confidence, and coaching—are important leadership qualities. I try to apply all three 3 C's by first setting the example. Continuous improvement is hard work, but it's also exciting and rewarding. People developers are the leaders who make a difference. My goal is to help people find the spark, the excitement, to engage in lifelong learning and growth.

—Ayn La Plant
President
Beekley Corporation

▲

Case Study—Applying the 3-C Leadership Model

At Veeder-Root we challenge people by first establishing a strategic plan for the entire business. Next, stretch goals that tie back to the strategic plan are flowed down to all employees. Everyone has aggressive targets to meet. In addition, individuals and teams are challenged to explain why key milestones aren't being met. For example, if a team is behind schedule, it might be asked, "What went wrong? What corrective actions will be taken? How will you get back on track?" We hold people accountable, which affirms our confidence that they can and will succeed. We also let teams know that senior management is willing to help. Sometimes it means temporarily moving resources to help a team get back on track.

Our managers and leaders build confidence in people by helping them succeed. Success builds confidence. They also reward and recognize effort and accomplishment. Our group executive is a hard-driving, results-oriented leader. He's also a tremendous cheerleader. It's not unusual for him to send out an e-mail to the entire organization praising individuals and teams when they hit their targets or do something special.

We coach our employees in a couple of different ways. Employees needing technical skills are sent to external training programs. In the management/ leadership area we do some training, but we need to do more. I also believe that some amount of teaching and coaching occurs in every meeting. People willingly share their ideas and insights and provide guidance on new ways of looking at problems and opportunities. Every meeting I attend, I try to walk away with at least one new idea.

If you're missing any one of the 3 Cs (challenge, confidence, coaching), growth and development won't occur. Effective leaders provide the right mix of the 3 Cs, and that's what helps people continue to improve.

—Janice Deskus
Former Director, Human Resources
Veeder-Root

PART III
Building Confidence

Most people like security and predictability. They like having clear goals and reliable strategies to follow. Unfortunately, today's business doesn't fit this scenario. Change—unprecedented, rapid change—is today's constant. Order, predictability, job security, and other entitlements are gone. Chaos seems to be the norm. Every day is a challenge to add value, accomplish more, work better and faster, and make sure the customer is "totally delighted." The challenges get bigger and tougher. Ray Kurlak, former president of Hamilton Standard, Division of United Technologies, Inc., made the point well in a pamphlet describing company strategy. He stated:

> Everything we do is measured against increasingly tougher standards. Deliveries must be to the day. Defects must be at the parts per million. Prices must decrease yearly. Products must do more and be more reliable.

When facing monumental challenges, many people begin to question and doubt their knowledge, skills, and abilities. "Do I have what it takes?" "Can I accomplish these agressive goals?" Their self-doubt often leads to a self-fulfilling prophecy. For example, an effective sales representative was promoted to a management position. After six months on the job, he stated, "My self-esteem was dropping. I didn't know how to manage people. My competence was selling, not managing. Because I had low self-esteem, I functioned even worse." At other times the increased pressure to do more faster pushes people deeper into their foxholes and creates more resistance to change. When adversity occurs, such as layoffs, diminishing profits, and new competition, self-confidence becomes a highly valued commodity. People need self-confidence to face and deal with difficult problems.

The best leaders help people believe in themselves. Perhaps the most critical leadership factor needed today is making people believe that "they have what it takes," that "they can do it!"

Listen to what these leaders say about confidence:

Jan Carlzon, the legendary CEO of Scandinavian Airline Systems (SAS), states that a leader's most important role is to instill confidence in people. People aren't born with self-confidence. Even after people develop self-confidence, they can lose it. Self-confidence comes from success, experience, and an organization's culture.

Tom Phillips, former president of Dynamic Controls/HS, Inc., states, "Today there is tremendous pressure on cost and schedule. People need to know you have confidence in them to make decisions and take action in response to these pressures. In addition, people need confidence to speak up and question current practices or proposed solutions to problems."

Will Schutz, corporate consultant and trainer, states, "How I feel about myself is the basic determinant of most of my behavior. When I improve my self-esteem, I will find that dozens of behaviors change automatically. If, for example, I increase my feeling of self-competence, I will probably be less defensive, less angered by criticism, less devastated if I don't get a raise. Confidence also makes me less afraid of making decisions, and more able to appreciate and praise other people."

People tend to rise to the occasion when someone truly believes in them. All great leaders find a way to believe in people's talent, abilities, and hidden potential. Successful leaders know that little can be accomplished if people don't feel capable and confident. On the other hand, those leaders who constantly demean people and find fault with their performance soon will be leading no one.

THE 3C LEADERSHIP MODEL

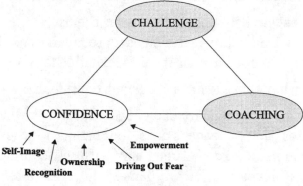

Figure III-1

The following are techniques leaders can use to build confidence in their associates (see figure III-1):

- Expand People's Self-Image
- Keep Ownership Where It Belongs
- Empower Your People
- Recognize Good or Improved Performance
- Drive Out Fear

CHAPTER 8
Expand People's Self-Image

How can leaders influence their associates' thinking to handle difficult challenges, such as increasing productivity by 35 percent or cutting cost by 40 percent? Many managers try to influence their employees by talking about the work. They explain what needs to be done, how important it is, that it probably isn't as hard to do as they might think, and so on. This approach often doesn't produce the desired result because knowing *what* needs to be done is only part of the equation. Having the confidence and ability to complete the job is something quite different. A leader's real hope lies in improving a person's self-image and building self-confidence. Helping people to believe in themselves and their abilities is an important prerequisite of success. During his baseball career, Reggie Jackson was once asked what made a great manager, and I think his response clearly illustrates this point. Jackson said, "I'll tell you what makes a great manager: A great manager has a knack for making ballplayers think they are better than they are. He forces you to have a good opinion of yourself. He lets you know he believes in you. He makes you get more out of yourself. And once you learn how good you really are, you never settle for playing anything less than your best."

Self-image is the accumulation of the thoughts, attitudes, and opinions that a person has about himself or herself. It begins in childhood and is based on our life experiences and the messages we receive from our parents, family members, friends, teachers, and coaches. Self-image impacts a person's confidence and sets the boundaries for individual accomplishments. People cannot consistently perform in a manner that is inconsistent with the way they see themselves. As a participant in one of my leadership seminars stated, "It is nearly impossible to achieve step-change improvements while possessing low self-confidence. Expand a person's confidence and you expand what's possible." (See figure 8.1.) To succeed, people need a positive self-image and a "can do" attitude.

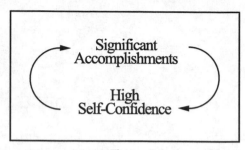

Figure 8.1

Here are several actions leaders can take to build people's self-image and confidence:

1. Let them succeed. You can build self-esteem and self-image by creating opportunities to be successful. Mary Jean Thornton, former president of Busy B Ice Cream, states: "Certainly you want to challenge people, but you also need to provide the required support. Then it's up to them to execute, to perform. Each success builds a stronger 'I can' attitude. Then, over time, the person needs fewer and fewer resources."

2. Make positive statements. Frequent sincere statements, such as "I'm confident in your abilities" or "I believe you have the skills and drive for this assignment," help to build self-esteem and confidence. Donna Shaw, contracts manager for Dynamic Controls/HS, Inc., HS, states, "I always got a confidence boost when my boss or a colleague said, 'You're the best we have for this assignment' or 'Other members of the team will greatly benefit from your experience.'"

3. Discuss new possibilities. Some leaders have the ability to motivate people to see themselves performing in a new, bigger role. This is accomplished by asking questions or making comments such as the following:

- "I can see you leading our international marketing campaign."
- "Consider what you would do if you were in charge of Northeast Operations."

4. Seek employee involvement. Asking people for their ideas and suggestions is an expression of a leader's confidence in them. Bill Devaney, former president of Stanley-Vidmar, says that soliciting employee involvement is an expression of confidence. It recognizes the ability and self-worth of each person and provides the opportunity for people to make meaningful contributions to their job, department, and company.

5. Demonstrate confidence. When a manager asks a subordinate to represent the group at a very important meeting, the underlying message is "I have confidence in you!" A product manager of a new car program showed confidence in his employees by not micromanaging and always looking over people's shoulders. Some leaders demonstrate their confidence in people by letting them present their ideas to the next higher level of management.

6. Remind people of their previous successes. Sometimes people forget or overlook some of their previous successes. One manager I know has his employees keep a running list of their accomplishments and periodically look them over—especially when they need a jolt of confidence. He states, "My people know they can succeed because I remind them they have done it before. They also want to succeed because I remind them how good they felt when they succeeded in the past."

7. Provide encouragement. One of my mentors was a great believer in encouragement. Whether I was applying for a new job, considering graduate school, or starting my own business, her consistent response was "Go for it." A first-line supervisor states, "Early in my career, a speech teacher sensed my feelings of self-doubt. She believed in me, coached me, and encouraged me. She proved that she cared about me as a person."

On a regular basis, as well as before assigning a difficult task, leaders need to build people's confidence and self-esteem. A senior manager states, "Even the best performers need an occasional pat on the back: 'You can do it' or 'You're on the track to reach the target.'" When a leader shows confidence in people, they begin to have confidence in themselves.

Conclusion—Expand People's Self-Image

Several years ago my former employer, the Hamilton Standard Division of United Technologies Corporation, was implementing a new flexible benefits program. Small group meetings were scheduled to explain the program's options to approximately five thousand salaried employees. Twenty-five people were trained to present the flexible benefits program information at these meetings. Cara, one of the program's administrators, had not made many presentations and hated the thought of standing in front of twenty employees. "I get so nervous; I won't be effective; I won't explain the information correctly." Stephani Cummings, benefits manager, met privately with Cara and stated, "I know this isn't your favorite activity, but I know you can be successful." Stephani affirmed her confidence in Cara. She went on to say, "I have a plan that will help you be successful." Stephani coached Cara on how to prepare for the presentations and critiqued several dry runs. She also arranged for Cara to meet with one of the company trainers, who provided additional coaching on the fine points of making effective presentations and guidance on how to handle hostile questions. The coaching and practice sessions made Cara feel more skilled, prepared, and confident. Cara successfully made twelve presentations. Actually, during the next year she became quite comfortable and proficient giving presentations to small groups of employees. Cara's performance improvement started when Stephani expressed confidence in her ability to succeed. As leaders show confidence and provide appropriate training, employees begin to trust in their ability to learn, grow, and have a positive impact.

Leaders help others discover their own inner greatness.

—handwritten message on a yellow Post-It note above the desk of a
human resource manager

CHAPTER 9
Keep Ownership Where It Belongs

The Romans had an interesting practice regarding ownership. After building an arch, the engineer in charge was expected to stand beneath it as the scaffolding was removed. If the arch didn't hold, he was the first to know. Effective leaders also keep ownership where it belongs. Holding people accountable sends a very important message. It says you have confidence in their abilities and skills; you have confidence they will successfully complete the assigned task.

Not holding people accountable when they don't perform parts of their job is an unwise practice. A middle manager states, "Giving people every chance to experience success and holding them accountable for results are very affirming practices. You are affirming your belief in their abilities."

Confidence and self-esteem are not feelings a leader confers on an employee. Rather, confidence develops as people take action, make mistakes, learn, grow, and accomplish their goals. Small

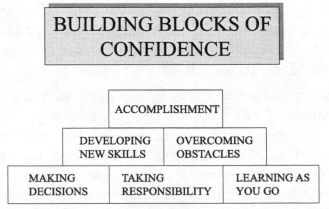

Figure 9-1

successes lead to bigger successes and more confidence. People feel good about themselves in proportion to their accomplishments. (See figure 9.1.) After successfully completing a very tough work assignment, an associate of mine stated, "I had a wonderful sense of accomplishment. My confidence level increased significantly. I was proud of my accomplishment and felt like I'd made a difference."

There are three pitfalls leaders face in keeping ownership where it belongs:

- Reverse delegation.

- The temptation to actually do the work.

- The blaming of another person or group.

The first pitfall is reverse delegation. It occurs when an employee gives work back to a leader. The employee may lack the ability, or confidence to do the work and therefore tries to give it back. Reverse delegation is often done by flattering the boss: "I can't do this. You're the expert; can you handle it?"

In cases where the employee lacks confidence, making decisions feels especially threatening. Therefore, the employee tends to escalate all decision making up the ladder. In these situations, the boss's ego is flattered, and he or she willingly takes on the task, makes the decision, or solves the problem. Ralph C. Stayer, CEO of Johnsonville Foods, says that the people responsible for a particular operation should make the decisions. Effective leaders support and encourage people to make decisions and take action as needed. As people gain experience in analyzing problems and making decisions, their confidence level rises.

The trap in becoming a *hero manager* is that every time you "pull a rabbit out of a hat," you generate more dependency from your subordinates. Astute leaders encourage their people to discuss problems and solutions but never let them leave their problems with the leader. As a reminder of this principle, one of the chief engineers at the Hamilton Standard Division of United Technologies Corporation has the following quote on his wall: "Remember, at no time during our discussion will your problem become mine. If that happens, then you don't have a problem, and I can't help anyone who doesn't have a problem."

A second pitfall some leaders face is the temptation to actually do the work (engineering, accounting, sales) they are supposed to be managing or leading. These leaders like certain work so much, they can't resist being personally involved. Also, in any type of crisis, these leaders are quick to jump in and start doing the work: "I'm the expert; I can get it done faster and better than anyone else." Their self-esteem is based on personal performance rather than staff performance. However, when leaders actually do the work, it negatively impacts their associates, who don't gain the experience they need to mature and grow. The leader's job isn't to do the hands-on work but rather to assign challenging responsibilities and coach employees to achieve desired results. A vice president states, "A critical part of a leader's job is to train and develop subordinates. I'm not developing my staff if I'm doing the work for them."

A third situation where leaders needs to keep ownership where it belongs occurs when employees try to blame another person or group for their own poor performance. In situations like this, people don't have to face and deal with their own shortcomings. For example, Joyce, an employee in a financial department, blames her lack of progress in implementing a new pricing system on the limited support and cooperation she's received. "The data processing department hasn't given me the data I need. It's holding me back. The department is not a team player." In this example, Joyce doesn't accept any personal responsibility for the lack of progress.

Within today's complex business environment, there are many interdependent relationships. Lack of cooperation and support among groups can and will cause problems. However, "pointing the finger" at other groups may be a convenient cover-up for not executing one's own responsibilities. Leaders need to unravel who is responsible for what. Who is performing and not performing? An organizational consultant states, "Think about top business leaders like Jack Welch, Bill Gates, and T. J. Rodgers. They have high performance standards and hold people accountable for results. They recognize the ability and talents of each person to make significant contributions."

Keeping ownership where it belongs is vital for an effectively run organization. Getting trapped in the pitfalls mentioned above doesn't help people gain the skills and confidence needed for success. When leaders accept nothing but the best, it affirms their confidence in people's ability to perform at the "A" level.

Conclusion—Keep Ownership Where It Belongs

Doris Brooks had been a secretary for over ten years at a small research and development company. During the past year she had been bounced around to several different assignments. After reductions in the human resources (HR) department, she was given responsibility to spend 50 percent of her time as the company's training coordinator. However, she had no experience in training. Her initial reaction was "I can't do this. I know nothing about training." The HR manager indicated his confidence in her by saying, "Doris, you're able to learn quickly. You have knowledge of the company and good administrative and interpersonal skills." The HR manager coached her on the key tasks and responsibilities of a training coordinator, including

- conducting needs assessment,
- selecting trainers,
- scheduling training sessions, and
- measuring effectiveness.

He also helped her think through the first two significant decisions that had to be made. However, when Doris went to him thereafter to "make decisions" that were rightly hers to make, he said, "As training coordinator, you need to make that decision. It's your decision." In essence, he held her accountable and in doing so was affirming his confidence in her. The HR manager states, "The first time I told Doris she had to make the decision, she was surprised, but deep down she was pleased. As she made decisions, her confidence grew. She found that many of her skills were transferable to the new tasks." Holding people accountable to make their own decisions says you have a lot of faith in their abilities. Successful leaders believe in people's enormous capacity to achieve what they attempt to do.

The buck stops with me, the process owner.

—sign on the desk of a project planning coordinator at a large manufacturing company

CHAPTER 10
Empower Your People

Most weekdays I go out to lunch with a group of three to five colleagues. When ordering, one of my usual questions is, "Can I get a cup of soup and a half sandwich?" This option is normally not on the menu. The reasons I ask this question are (1) that's what I want and (2) I'm seeing to what extent the waiter or waitress is empowered to satisfy a customer. Unfortunately, the answer I have consistently received is something like "Oh, no, that's not on the menu; you have to get a whole sandwich" or "I'd have to check with the manager, but I don't think he will allow it." We've all heard a lot of talk about empowerment, but to what extent are people really given authority to make decisions and take action? A bank teller in a branch office told me, "I'm really embarrassed when a customer wants to cash a check and I have to ask him to wait while I get it approved by my manager." Lack of empowerment not only frustrates customers, it also frustrates employees. Lack of empowerment means "I don't have confidence in your abilities and judgment to make the correct decisions." (See figure 10.1.)

EMPOWERMENT

What people say after being empowered with responsibility and authority:

- "Terrific! I feel people believe in me."
- "People have confidence in my skills."
- "My boss trusts me to make the right decisions."
- "I don't have to ask permission."
- "I'm eager to show what I can do and happy to know people have faith in me."

Figure 10.1

Not only is it okay for the buck to stop lower in the organization, it's necessary. Competition requires decisions to be made quickly by people closest to customers and suppliers. A leader who must review and approve all decisions quickly becomes a bottleneck in the organization. At some large companies, nothing gets done unless five people sign paperwork to approve the decision. Requiring multiple sign-offs and second-guessing people's decisions indicate a lack of confidence in people's judgement. This not only wastes a lot of time, but also no one person is held accountable for decisions or action taken. Leaders need to let go of some authority and empower their associates. Effective leaders have great confidence in people. They demonstrate their confidence by giving people the authority, information, and resources they need to manage their part of the business.

It's important to remember that responsibility without authority doesn't work. The best leaders don't just make people *feel* like owners or *feel* important, they make people *be* owners and *be* important parts of the business. In his book *The Great Game of Business*, Jack Stack states that people need to think like owners, not employees. Real owners have the knowledge and information needed to make decisions. In addition, they have the motivation and will to act fast. According to Stack, hourly associates at his company, Springfield Remanufacturing Corporation, make statements like the following: "Cash flow is projected to increase by $25K this month." "Operating income was $85K, which represents a 3.3 percent return on sales." How is this possible? The answer is easy—the associates have been educated to understand the financial rules of the business. In addition, they receive regular feedback on a number of financial measures. To make intelligent decisions, people need financial information as well as feedback from the customer. Are they satisfied? What are their complaints?

Naturally, the amount of power and authority given to a person depends on his or her business experience. Gradually, more and more responsibility and authority should be given as people gain experience and receive training. Too much empowerment or empowerment without the proper training can cause serious problems. As one experienced leader stated, "People need to be challenged. You need to give people enough responsibility and authority so they're always a bit outside their comfort zone. However, you can't give an inexperienced person control over a $50 million budget."

Helping people understand organizational goals, values, and beliefs provides them with a framework in which to exercise their power. Today's leader needs to be a coach and teacher helping employees run their parts of the business. Leaders need to support and encourage their people to make decisions and take action as needed. Once people are empowered, leaders must be disciplined in *not* making decisions that rightfully should be made at lower levels in the organization. For example, when people ask you to make decisions they should be making, what do you do? A middle manager in one of my seminars stated, "Don't jump in and rescue them." You may want to ask questions and facilitate the discussion, but don't make the decision. When you give people responsibility and authority, make sure they use it.

As employees use their authority to make decisions and achieve results, their confidence grows. Experience produces both successes and failures—ideally, people learn from both. One executive states, "Confidence is a by-product of learning—learning how to define and solve problems, learning new skills, learning how to view mistakes as lessons learned."

Empowerment is really about helping people gain the knowledge, skills, and authority to act like business owners. Here are some additional suggestions to accomplish that goal:

1. **Have people meet with customers on a regular basis.** Real business owners spend a lot of time with their customers. Listening to customers and getting their feedback is critical. In addition, share customer letters and surveys with everyone.

2. Let people see the financials. How can you expect people to think and act like business owners if they don't know what's happening with sales and costs?

3. Give people the quality and operational data they need, such as productivity, scrap, rework, and inventory reports.

4. Don't interfere. Let people who are running their parts of the business make the decisions.

Conclusion—Empowerment

My wife, Mary Jean, owned a soft ice cream store, which operated from April 15 through Labor Day. Both of our children, Kate and Andy, worked there during the summer months. After they had worked there a few weeks, Mary Jean made this comment to each of them: "You'll often be working by yourself. I have confidence you can handle the job. You also have the power to do whatever is needed to satisfy the customer. However, you're also responsible for managing costs. We need to make a profit." Both children were coached on what it means to be "customer focused" and were educated on various costs such as supplies, electricity, and inventory. Up until that point, Kate and Andrew had little concern about the cost side of the equation. For example, they would give customers ten napkins when they needed only one. Mary Jean gave the children monthly feedback on both sales and various costs. Over a two-year period, costs were reduced by 28 percent and sales increased approximately 12 percent. Leaders like Mary Jean have confidence in people's abilities. They demonstrate their confidence by giving people real authority to make decisions and take action as needed.

Do what you think best....Not what you think I'll think.

—sign in the office of Jeno F. Paulucci, CEO, Luigino's Foods

▲

CHAPTER 11
Recognize Good or Improved Performance

Another way leaders can develop confident people is by rewarding and recognizing good or improved performance. Many companies give employees various rewards—for example, time off, movie tickets or weekend getaways—for achieving significant goals. Certainly most people, including myself, like receiving these types of rewards. However, in my opinion, what's far more important than the reward is the recognition that accompanies the reward (see figure 11.1).

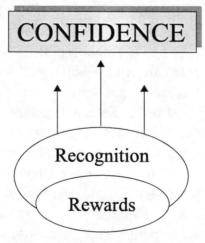

Figure 11.1

By that I mean the words spoken by an authority figure when the reward is presented. These words can have a lasting impact on a person's self-esteem and confidence. Research has shown that a pay increase has a motivational impact only for about two weeks. I believe words that are personalized, thoughtful, uplifting, and direct can have an impact for a lifetime.

For example, one of my colleagues received an award for "outstanding management effectiveness." She states, "I was very happy to be chosen for this award. The plaque and the twenty-five hundred dollar award were great, but what really made it special were the compliments my boss gave me when he presented the award. He said I had made the difference in our winning the Bell contract. It was obvious he valued me as a person and a professional. I felt his confidence and trust in me. His comments have made a lasting impression."

In one of my leadership seminars I asked the participants to answer the question, "What types of compliments about your performance have the biggest impact on you?" Responses included the following:

- "When the compliment is real. When it's obvious the person giving the compliment truly values what I did."

- "When the compliment is personalized about what I specifically did."

- "If the compliment is thoughtful and sincere, it's special."

- "Compliments from my customers are the best and most valued."

- "When recognition is delivered with passion and enthusiasm."

When leaders recognize people, they are really saying "I noticed." They have noticed "better quality," "lower cost," "improved teamwork," "faster response time," and so on. It's also important to recognize or acknowledge "effort." Many people are working twelve-to-fifteen-hour days to achieve stretch goals. It's very important for leaders to acknowledge this level of commitment.

When you acknowledge and recognize effort and/or results, I recommend that you follow the what, how, and why technique. Describe what the person or team did, how it was done, and why it's significant. Be specific. Generalities are not nearly as effective as specifics. For example, if a leader states, "That was a great meeting you ran," the receiver will feel good but may also be wondering what exactly made it great.

Here are some other points to keep in mind regarding rewards and recognition:

- **Focus on results and skills.** One executive states, "I try to not only recognize what people accomplished but also highlight the unique skills and special talents they used to be successful."

- **How you say it is important.** A senior management trainer states, "The words used to recognize performance are important. But maybe even more important is how the message is delivered. Factors such as eye contact, handshake, smiling, and enthusiasm are critical."

- **Don't overlook people who quietly and effectively do their jobs.** Recently, during lunch at a local restaurant I spoke with a person who had been a dishwasher for three years. She knew her process and consistently produced quality results. However, she had never received recognition for a job well done.

- **Expand your praise vocabulary.** Ronald E. Guzik, president, Entrepreneurial Visions, says that the words "nice" and "good" are overused when giving praise or recognition. Using words such as "excellent," "complete," "creative," "innovative," "leading edge," "breakthrough thinking," and "wonderful" can have a more meaningful impact on the receiver.

- **Praise yourself.** When I play tennis I frequently hear players criticizing themselves for poor shots. I seldom hear them praise themselves when they make good shots. If you can't praise yourself, how can you praise others? I've noticed that high achievers openly praise themselves for their accomplishments.

Remember, you will find what you look for, so look for the positive.

Conclusion—Recognize Good or Improved Performance

Donna DeCaro Conley, one of my high-achieving colleagues, said she remembers receiving recognition and positive feedback many times throughout her career. These positive acknowledgments affirmed her skills and built her self-confidence. However, Donna vividly remembers three occasions when she received positive reinforcement that elevated her confidence to a new level. The three events were as follows:

1. Donna was given a major project to complete in a short period of time. Most people in the department felt it was impossible to meet the aggressive schedule. Somehow, by working day and night and effectively using two support people, Donna completed the project on schedule. She states, "My boss recognized me in front of my peers. He said, 'I didn't think you could pull this off. I really thought this was going to fail.' Her boss followed these comments with lots of praise and positive remarks. Donna states, "I think this experience was special and impactful because no one really thought I could meet the schedule."

2. A second occasion was special because of who was providing the recognition. She was given positive reinforcement by an executive she respected and considered an expert. Donna states, "Receiving recognition from someone I thought walked on water made me almost feel like a peer. It was special. I still remember how I felt."

3. The third situation had to do with a team Donna led over a six-month period. She was responsible for a tedious and time-consuming project that people had to do in addition to their regular tasks. When the project was completed, the team sent her a dozen roses with a note that stated, "Without your leadership, we never would have finished this project." She says, "This not only made me feel great, it gave me the confidence to take on bigger challenges."

Kind words can be short and easy to speak
but their echoes are truly endless.

—Mother Teresa

CHAPTER 12
Drive Out Fear

Many businesses have gone through extensive layoffs, acquisitions, mergers, reorganizations, and reengineering initiatives. Constant change has increased the level of fear in many organizations. Adding to that fear is the new "employment contract" that basically says to employees, "We can't guarantee you lifetime employment. You're responsible for managing your career and keeping your skills up-to-date." When people are constantly worried and afraid, they stay in their comfort zones. People are afraid to speak up and be risk-takers.

When people are motivated by fear, common reactions include:

- *Preoccupation:* "I'm so worried about my job status, I can't concentrate."

- *Paranoia:* "I think everyone's out to get me."

- *Rigidity:* "I'm hanging on to what I know."

- *Conservativeness:* "I'm only going to do what I'm told to do."

- *Self-Absorbtion:* "I'm watching out for number one."

Obviously, people with these attitudes don't embrace change. Fear causes inertia. Talk substitutes for action because that's safe and easy. Today, companies need confident people who view change as an exciting opportunity. To achieve big, bold improvements, people must be willing to leave their comfort zones and try totally new and sometimes radical ways of working. Remember that Sam Walton's greatest strength was his fearlessness. He'd make a blunder on Monday. On Tuesday he'd show up raring to go, eager to try something new.

How do some leaders react to fear in the workplace? Some deny it exists. Others acknowledge it and simply hope it will go away. Another way some leaders react to fear and uncertainty is by acting tough: "You need to be thankful you have a job and get on with implementing the new system!" Acting tough does nothing to reduce employees' fear. Rather, it shuts down the communication process and leads to "happy talk" at best.

Dr. W. Edwards Deming developed fourteen points managers and leaders must follow to achieve quality results. Point 8 states, "Drive out fear so that everyone may work effectively for the company." Fear often causes people to stop thinking creatively and to cover up problems. Think about this cycle (see figure 12.1): When people are afraid, they hide and cover up their mistakes. This in turn prohibits any new learning from occurring. If people aren't learning and growing, they don't gain the skills and confidence needed to face new challenges.

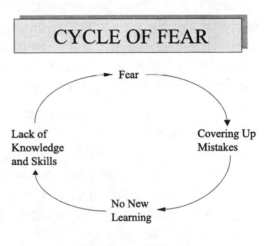

Figure 12.1

Dr. Deming was opposed to all techniques managers use to motivate employees by fear. People who are afraid don't want to change. They want to keep doing what's familiar, even if the product quality is poor. An operations director states, "Fear makes people stay in their foxholes. Businesses need people who will aggressively climb out of their foxholes even when the bullets are flying. That takes confidence. Believing in yourself is critical." Managers and leaders take several steps to drive out fear:

1. Explain what and why. Fear is defined as an unpleasant, strong emotion caused by anticipation or awareness of danger. When people lack information and understanding, they feel anxious and powerless.

They often assume that change will make them ever more powerless. Leaders who help people understand not only what is happening but why it is happening are providing the information that will help employees react in a mature, adult fashion.

2. Communicate honestly. Give people the truth. Fear is often brought about by a lack of knowledge of what's going to happen in the future. Honest, open, and frequent information helps people see an accurate picture of the present and future direction the company is taking. This means presenting both the good and the bad news. In the absence of current information, employees have a tendency to fill in the gaps with their own assumptions, often based on worst-case scenarios. One executive states, "The needs of people and the business are best met with open, candid communication. If we always act in a 'tough love' fashion, people will know they can believe what we say."

3. Acknowledge fear and insecurity. Especially during periods of layoffs, mergers, or other major changes, leaders need to acknowledge people's feelings of fear and insecurity. Leaders shouldn't dwell on these emotions, but discussing them often clears the air. One outplacement expert says, "People aren't emotionally prepared to handle major disruptions. You have to help employees adapt to the changing world of work. Allowing them to express their negative feelings and discontent is a good first step."

4. Upgrade knowledge and skills. The more up-to-date knowledge and skills people have, the less afraid they are to deal with change. Ongoing education and training help people feel more prepared, more confident. Leaders need to provide learning opportunities such as cross-training, understudy assignments, special projects, seminars, workshops, and college courses.

5. Encourage preparation. The more prepared people feel, the less afraid they feel. Being prepared means you have done your homework and you're ready to compete. One of my colleagues states, "When you're prepared, you don't have the nervousness that can distract you. Preparation gives you the confidence to aggressively pursue your goals and strategy."

6. Focus on the positive. Every risk has an upside and a downside. Focusing on the downside often leads to uncertainty and fear, while concentrating on the upside creates the energy and motivation needed to succeed. Denis Waitley, author of *The New Dynamics of Winning,* says that champions focus their thoughts and energy on the desired result. They are propelled toward that goal by desire, not inhibited by fear.

7. Don't punish risktakers. If people are really taking significant risks, they are going to make mistakes or fail to achieve desired goals. Michael Eisner, CEO of Walt Disney, says that companies must create an atmosphere in which people feel it's safe to fail. This means creating an organization where failure is tolerated and fear of criticism for submitting a foolish idea is abolished.

8. Stop shooting the messenger. At a lot of companies, the person who delivers bad news gets "killed" by the manager: "Did Joe say that? He's gone." In this type of environment, employees become afraid to speak up. Who wants to be the one to tell the boss the sales plan won't work? Leaders need to be receptive to bad news. Appreciate those employees who courageously report problems, complaints, and concerns.

9. Some fear may be healthy. In an October 14, 1996, *Fortune* article by Kenneth Labich, Andy Grove, CEO of Intel, said that top management should infuse people with a passion to win in the marketplace. Fear of the competition plays a major role in creating and maintaining such passion. This type of fear motivates people to constantly think about and look for new ideas, new strategies, and new rules to play the game.

Conclusion—Drive Out Fear

At many companies annual performance appraisals are fraught with fear. People often dread going to that thirty-minute meeting to discuss how they performed over the past six or twelve months.

I have heard comments like the following:

- "I hate having a performance appraisal. My boss focuses only on what I did wrong."

- "I spend half my time on teams; my supervisor has no idea what I do."

- "I never had any written objectives, so how can I be held accountable? It's unfair."

Many people refer to their performance appraisals as getting their report cards, which produced some anxious moments when they were students. To help drive out fear and empower people, one leader said the following to her direct reports:

"At the end of the year I will allow each of you to write your own performance appraisal. I will make no changes to your self-assessment. I will give you clear expectations and feedback throughout the year. But it will be up to each of you to write your own performance appraisal."

Taking this action was a major step in empowering her staff members to evaluate their own performance, and in addition, it drove out fear. People were relieved to know that their appraisals would be fair and accurate because they themselves would be completing them. One direct report stated, "I was always a bit worried about how I'd be rated. Now I have complete confidence in the system." The supervisor stated that this appraisal system was a small but important step in making people less fearful, and it showed her confidence in their professionalism. The approach worked quite well. The leader spent her time setting expectations, defining standards of excellence, and giving timely performance feedback. She found that people were very fair and realistic in rating themselves. Actually, two direct reports were a lot tougher assessing themselves than the leader would have been.

It's impossible for people to be creative and innovative if they are afraid or upset. "Driving out fear" is the necessary first step to creating an environment where people can be creative. Today it's hard to find business situations where you don't need creativity and a high energy level from all your employees. Effective leaders drive out fear so everyone can contribute their best performance.

When you're well prepared, you're not scared.

—sign on the office wall of Stew Leonard, Jr., President, Stew Leonard's Dairy

SUMMARY
Building Confidence

Below is a list of leaders who took the initiative in building people's confidence. They may have used different approaches, but their common aim was to help people to believe in themselves. They found a way to highlight people's abilities, skills, and untapped potential.

Mary Kay, founder and leader of the Mary Kay Cosmetics Company, grew her company from a tiny storefront operation in Dallas into an international multimillion-dollar corporation. A key part of her success had to do with building salespeople's confidence through reward, recognition, attention, and appreciation. Whenever she met someone, she'd try to imagine the person wearing an invisible sign that says "Make Me Feel Important." She then would do whatever it took to make the person feel special and important.

Tom Phillips, former president, Dynamic Controls/HS, Inc., had skip level meetings every two weeks with fifteen to twenty employees. (Senior managers hold meetings with employees who are two or more levels below them in the organization.) At the end of every meeting he would tell the group members how proud he was of them, how much confidence he had in their abilities, and how much he valued what they were doing.

Donald Petersen, former chairman and CEO of Ford Motor Company, made it a practice to write a positive message to one or more of his associates every day. He said, "I'd just scribble them on a memo pad or the corner of a letter and pass them along. The most important ten minutes of your day are those you spend doing something to boost the people who work for you."

Jack Welch, former CEO of General Electric, is a big believer in the importance of self-confidence throughout an organization. He says that companies cannot distribute self-confidence. What companies must do is to give each of its people the opportunity to dream, risk, and achieve success. Self-confidence is earned.

Ralph Stayer, former CEO of Johnsonville Foods, built confidence in his workforce by transferring total responsibility and ownership to the people doing the work. He says that people who are responsible should make the decisions—you don't have to be responsble if someone else is making decisions for you. Leadership is about helping people regain their own authority and power to respond to problems at work and in life.

Jack Canfield has helped many people develop confidence and self-esteem through his books, audio, and video programs. His training and educational programs provide numerous examples of the specific actions people have taken to overcome obstacles, gain confidence, and achieve great success. Jack is the author and narrator of several audio and video programs, including "Self-Esteem and Peak Performance."

All of these leaders have helped build people's confidence and self-esteem. They used a variety of approaches, but their goal was similar. Help people develop the "I can do it" self-confidence required for success.

Case Studies—Applying the 3-C Leadership Model

Chapters 8–12 described numerous ways that leaders build and strengthen people's self-confidence. In addition to building people's self-confidence, effective leaders challenge people to pursue bigger goals and objectives. They also coach people in how to reach their goals. The following case studies describe how Don Sweet and Steve Chanin apply the **3-C Leadership Model**. Don is vice president of finance for Siebe Pneumatics and Steve is director of operations for ABB Corporation.

▲

Case Study—Applying the 3-C Leadership Model

Before applying the 3 C Leadership Model (challenge, confidence, and coaching), it's important to understand the needs of one's business. What challenges does the business face? What strategies are being implemented? The answers to these types of big-picture questions give me a context in which to operate. In addition, it's important to have some understanding of the people. What are their goals and aspirations? Their strengths and weaknesses? Their definition of success?

One approach I use to challenge people is asking questions. Or sometimes I simply say, "Tell me more about XYZ issue." I want to understand how people are thinking about a particular issue. Their comments tell me how they define, analyze, and develop solutions. Their thought process follows a particular track with built-in assumptions. Questioning assumptions helps people see the value in evaluating whether the assumptions are still valid. In other cases, the right question can put people on a new, different track—a new way of seeing the issue.

I also use formal and informal performance reviews as a way to reward the good work but also as an opportunity to challenge people to improve their performance in specific areas. My job is to keep raising the performance bar.

People need self-confidence or a belief in themselves that they can perform with the best. I sometimes simply affirm my confidence in people. For example, one of our sales reps was facing a new, very demanding account. I said to him, "I know you can do this. I know you can get through to this client." Affirming words like these can mean a great deal. Another way I build people's confidence is by providing assignments in which they can excel. Throw a few softball pitches so people can hit home runs. Success produces a can-do attitude, a positive self-image. Sometimes big challenges need to be broken down into bite-size pieces. Let people succeed one bite at a time.

Helping people succeed often requires day-to-day coaching. I view my job as coach or mentor as being a "talking partner." I try to create situations where people can openly and candidly discuss their problems and ideas.

Coaching may mean redirecting their approach or it may mean facilitating a discussion. I also help people draw their own conclusions. In some situations coaching means finding the right resource to help people. For example, on a few occasions I hired an industrial psychologist. He helped several people develop more effective interpersonal skills. He also helped me to better understand and work with them.

I want and need capable and confident people who can handle global competition. Every day we face tough challenges that require new, creative solutions. Confident people are willing to step out of their comfort zones and test new ways of thinking and doing business. I have also learned that I must set a good example. I try to constantly challenge myself by taking courses and reading business journals. Every business event provides opportunities to learn. I'm always looking for the benchmark: Who's considered the best?

I view the 3 C Leadership Model as a tripod. Each leg of the tripod is one of the Cs—challenge, confidence, and coaching. At the top of the tripod is success. All three Cs are required for success. Effective leaders provide the right amount of each C to help people succeed and reach their goals.

—Don Sweet

Vice President, Finance
Siebe Pneumatics

Case Study—Applying the 3-C Leadership Model

I challenge people by letting them solve their own problems and by assigning them to teams—cross-functional Kaizen [a Japanese concept that means continuous improvement] teams that have specific improvement targets in the areas of quality, cycle time, and part travel distance. The teams are told they have five days to meet their targets; they need to take action now. It's up to the teams to figure out how to make it happen. They have full authority to make changes. When you give people complete ownership for reducing cycle time from three days to three hours, that's a challenge.

The first one and a half days people are getting acclimated to their new responsibilities. However, by the end of the week, all the changes and improvements are implemented. It's a real confidence boost when people have the authority to make changes and realize what they have accomplished. We also set up informal hourly/salary teams to attack everyday production problems. We make people feel more confident by giving them responsibility to manage their personal and work lives. Flextime has been implemented for hourly workers, and we have also removed the time clocks. We trust our employees. My goal is to treat everyone like a first-class citizen. We also reward and recognize people when they hit home runs or demonstrate outstanding effort. We have group activities such as "Bagel Day" and "Jamaican Patty Day" on Thursdays and "Fish and Chip Day" on Fridays.

I don't believe you can coach people until you have provided the other two pieces of the model—challenge and confidence. Coaching is about improving performance and solving conflicts. People do not have a need to improve until they are challenged, and without confidence they do not believe they can improve. For me, coaching often involves helping people understand the big picture. It's important that all the people understand the key business drivers, what they can control, and what is important to our customers. Coaching also involves helping people apply the theories and concepts they learn in the classroom. Understanding theory is only one part of the process; applying it on the job is another. Leaders cannot be effective coaches until they can be trusted. Even though leaders are coaches, they are still responsible for their areas and meeting all production requirements. Successful coaches must be highly skilled in solving personal conflicts between employees. Until the people issues are solved, coaching will not be effective.

Effective leaders are proficient at all three Cs—challenge, confidence, and coaching. These leadership actions properly executed create a culture in which people have ownership; feel excited, confident, enthusiastic, competent, and responsible; have input to their jobs; and enjoy coming to work. That is a great culture.

—Steve Chanin
Director, Operations
Asea Brown Boveri Corporation

PART IV
Coaching to Achieve Top Performance

In today's rapidly changing world with new technology, new ways of working, and broader jobs, people often need a coach, teacher, or mentor. Sometimes people simply need to make sense out of the changes that are occurring. Other times people need help in developing new skills or strategies. In these situations a leader must step forward and provide the required coaching. As a participant in one of my leadership seminars stated, "Coaching involves spending time with people on the job, day by day—talking about attitudes, concepts, goals, and strategies and providing people with direct feedback. Every interaction with employees is an opportunity to raise people's level of awareness and performance." Coaching and teaching are central activities of every successful leader.

One senior executive at a Fortune 100 company, speaking to an MBA class, stated the following:

> One very important person to find, listen to, and learn from is a mentor. Many successful people will say they had a mentor who played a key role and helped them at different stages of their career. My mentor encouraged me to take tough assignments, broaden my experience, and continuously update my skills. He coached me on the subtle aspects of management and organizational politics.

Don Shula, a former top coach in the National Football League, says that a coach asks performers to push their limits, which automatically means you'll often make unpopular requests. Top coaches and leaders inspire people to achieve more than they thought they could. Part of coaching is challenging people to perform at a higher level. Another aspect of coaching is building people's confidence that they can perform at a higher level. The third part of coaching involves teaching people how to think or act. For example, it may involve teaching a new attitude or viewpoint toward a new company initiative, such as safety or quality. Sometimes a person is simply asking, "Talk me through how you envision this 'customer focus' initiative." Coaching may also involve teaching someone a new skill, such as how to run a meeting or make a presentation. A big part of coaching is letting people practice and then providing helpful feedback.

Leaders use the following techniques to coach people to achieve top performance (see figure IV-1):

- Find the Right Balance
- Make People Think for Themselves
- Show People What Good Performance Looks Like
- Be a Facilitator
- Give Feedback

THE 3C LEADERSHIP MODEL

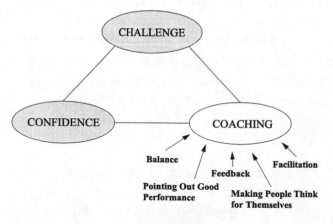

Figure IV-1

CHAPTER 13
Find the Right Balance

As previously stated, an important part of a leader's job is to coach people and provide guidance for them to be successful. However, one senior executive pointed out to me there's a slim difference between too little and too much guidance. Too much can frustrate initiative, like a parent who helps a child with homework so much it becomes the parent's homework, not the child's. The leader who provides excessive coaching and guidance often has a need to be needed. He or she thinks, "They can't do it without me—they need my direction." In one case, after ten months of being overcoached, the employee was unable to make the smallest work decision by herself without first consulting with her supervisor. Too much help, like "welfare programs," destroys people's initiative. It makes people dependent, and as their dependence grows, they increasingly doubt their skills and abilities.

On the other hand, too little coaching or guidance can cause excessive frustration and failure. Sometimes failure can be the best teacher. But other times it can be catastrophic, as in the case of an accident, injury, or loss of a major customer.

Not overcoaching is one quality that distinguishes good leaders from average ones. Sometimes people in leadership roles want so badly for their people to succeed that they do everything for them. That takes away people's chance to experiment, learn, grow, and develop. I like the quote by businessman J. C. Penney: "I'm grateful for all my problems. As each of them was overcome, I became stronger and more able to meet those yet to come. I grew in all my difficulties." Often our greatest growth occurs after we have wrestled and struggled with a problem. As one of my colleagues stated, "What you learn the hard way, after multiple tries and attempts, causes you to never forget the lesson. Those lessons create powerful imprints."

Effective coaches realize that each person is different, and what's appropriate for one may be overkill for another. A good question leaders need to ask themselves is, "What's the least amount of guidance this person needs to succeed?" Providing the least amount of guidance requires the person to show initiative to learn and grow.

One of my mentors, Bill Huber, formerly vice president of engineering at the Hamilton Standard Division of United Technologies Corporation, was excellent at not overcoaching. His staff meetings were memorable for the philosophical debates we had on many business issues. Bill solicited ideas from his staff and often challenged us to see issues from different points of view. In these debates Bill didn't try to supply all the answers. He coached us by framing the issues and leaving us to think through the consequences of our recommendations.

One of his common themes had to do with "balance": finding the right spot between two extremes. For example, "customer focus" is critical to competing in today's marketplace, but what happens at either end of the customer service continuum? If you provide too little service or the wrong kind, the customer will leave. On the other hand, if you provide too many options or service the customer isn't willing to pay for, your company may overspend or price itself out of the market. Bill coached us by asking questions and making comments such as, "If managers don't understand the cost side of the equation, they don't know where to draw the line on what they will do to satisfy the customer." The effective coach is always looking for that spot where he or she is providing help and assistance, but not too much. Bill's coaching methods made us think, question, debate, struggle, and develop our own conclusions.

Some coaches are very effective at designing learning events in which trainees observe or participate in a particular activity and then draw their own conclusions. The following are examples:

- An executive at a consumer products company was having trouble being an effective team leader. His mentor arranged for seats behind the coach at a basketball game. The executive's assignment was to watch the coach, study how he interacted with the team and the assistant coaches, and observe what the coach did that the executive didn't. The executive learned two things: 1) He had to listen to his team members before he spoke, and 2) when he spoke he needed to be more succinct.

- In a course titled "Leadership and Teamwork," students attended a regional stock car race. Their assignment was to observe the pit crew and discover three new insights about effective teamwork. Students walked away with new insights about common goals, clear roles, the interdependence of team members, speed of delivery, problem solving, and celebrating success.

Self-discovery learning is powerful because participants develop new insights when they see concrete examples of effective teamwork.

Some managers have asked me, "What makes the light bulb go on? What creates that teachable moment that leads to self-discovery?" I believe some of the coaching behaviors that create teachable moments and self-discovery learning are:

- Stopping the person at critical points and asking what they are doing/thinking and why.

- Balancing learning with unlearning. Helping the person discover what they need to unlearn.

- Teaching people to question and examine their behavior on a regular basis.

- Requiring alternate periods of participation and reflection.

- Requiring people to make connections. How does what they observed relate to their work environment?

People remember best the insights they discover, experience, and learn themselves. Good coaches structure events and utilize follow-up questions to reinforce learning.

Conclusion—Find the Right Balance

Author and philosopher Peter Koestenbaum believes leaders develop a keen understanding of the many paradoxes employees face including:

- courage versus fear,
- change versus staying the same,
- individual needs versus team needs, and
- career versus family issues.

Leaders help people work through these contradictions. Peter states, "Leaders must understand human nature, and, above all, be capable of entertaining dialogues about deep issues if called upon. Key is the ability to talk with depth about ethics, conflict and courage, which include empathy and principle in ethics and anxiety and free will in courage." According to Peter, coaching steps include:

- Helping people increase their understanding of who they are and what they believe in—what's important and what's not.

- Intelligent conversations focused on character building. Where do people draw the line in support of their values?

- Making it clear that they must make decisions relative to each paradox.

Leaders provide the right amount of coaching to help people understand and deal with these contradictions. Finding the "right balance" is an important concept. Providing too much or too little coaching is equally bad. The best leaders/coaches help people find their own answers to difficult questions. When this happens, people grow, develop, and become more independent.

**A leader's job is to help people, not judge them.
It is to know when people need special help, and provide it.
He is not a leader unless he does know.**

—W. Edwards Deming, Ph.D.

CHAPTER 14
Make People Think for Themselves

A senior executive states, "One of my best business teachers responded to all my questions by helping me answer them myself." An important part of coaching is helping people to think for themselves. It's not uncommon to hear leaders asking the following questions: "What's your opinion?" "What concerns do you have?" "How will you implement that strategy?" In my leadership seminars, participants often say that effective coaching involves helping people to see the consequences of taking a certain action. Leaders often ask questions that help people think through the cost/benefit ratios of implementing their recommendations. Socrates, one of the greatest teachers of all time, used one teaching methodology-he asked questions. He forced people to think. (See figure 14.1.)

SOCRATIC TEACHING

Ask questions that challenge people

- to think
- to analyze
- to make connections
- to probe for meaning
- to understand

Figure 14.1

One step leaders can take to help people think for themselves is to teach them basic financial concepts. Understanding financial concepts—for example, cost, budget, inventory, overhead rates, depreciation, and profit—is critical if employees are really running their own business. One manager states, "Our company is bringing in seminars that teach people the basics of accounting and finance so that they'll appreciate what impacts cost and profit." People need to understand financial concepts before they can learn how to keep inventories low and how to manage overhead expenses.

Assigning people to new jobs, rotating department assignments, and carrying out special projects are other ways to help people develop their thinking skills. For example, when someone rotates from the marketing department to the operations department, he or she is confronted with a whole new set of issues and problems to solve. These assignments broaden people's background and help them see the business from a different perspective. The best leaders rotate their top talent and make them available for new opportunities. They don't hide their top talent or have ready-made excuses why they can't release someone: "I can't transfer Sue, she's too critical to the success of the ZMZ program."

Brainstorming is another technique to get people thinking and tap their creative brainpower. In brainstorming sessions, people are asked for their suggestions on how to solve a specific problem. Brainstorming sessions have taught me the following:

1. Most people like being asked, "What do you think?"

2. There are many unique and different ways to solve a problem.

3. Building on the ideas of others often produces creative solutions.

4. Silence is okay-the best may be yet to come.

5. Creative thinking sometimes occurs when you let your mind wanders.

A facilitator usually records all ideas on a flipchart. Then similar recommendations are combined and finally evaluated. A management consultant states, "It is a sharing and learning event that normally produces better ideas, more effective solutions. In addition, when people develop their own solutions, they're eager to prove their solutions will work."

Leaders also help people think about and learn from their mistakes. Lessons-learned meetings are effective tools for continuous improvement. Asking questions and forcing people to pinpoint specific lessons learned are critical. What separates top leaders from average leaders is that the top leaders keep probing and digging until root-cause issues are identified. Specific lessons learned need to be shared and passed on to all employees who can benefit from this knowledge. In addition, documenting these lessons learned can be a big help for future reference. For example, within the design engineering group at the Hamilton Standard Division of United Technologies Corporation, lessons learned are kept in a database. Before designing new parts, engineers are required to review the appropriate lessons-learned section.

Perhaps the most important aspect of learning from mistakes is being open and honest. When people are defensive, little or no learning occurs. Meeting negative feedback with rationalizations or denial prevents growth and improvement. Leaders cannot mandate people to be open and receptive, but they can act as positive role models. When leaders welcome negative feedback, without getting defensive, they are setting a good example.

The more people are capable of thinking for themselves, the more prepared they are to face the constant change of business. Remember, the object of teaching is to enable the student to get along without a teacher. When people are capable of teaching themselves, they can be challenged to utilize their teaching skills to help other people grow and develop.

Conclusion—Make People Think for Themselves

Programs like those offered by OutwardBound force people to think for themselves. The typical program takes place in a remote area. Participants are faced with one or more challenges that require them to work as a team, be creative, and solve unique problems.

A few years ago, I attended a program called "The Executive Challenge." It was held in a very isolated, wooded section of New Hampshire. Ten people from the Hamilton Standard Division of United Technologies Corporation arrived at 3:00 p.m. on a Friday to attend the weekend program.

After discussing our objectives for the weekend and reviewing safety requirements, we embarked on our first task. Our challenge was to try to get as many people as possible to stand on a twelve-inch square that was four inches off the ground. We were given fifteen minutes to discuss and brainstorm how we might tackle this assignment. Our group did generate lots of creative ideas. However, after completing the assignment, our facilitator said, "Joe, you made a good suggestion on how to get more people standing on the box. Do you feel your group listened to you?" Joe answered, "No." Actually, several people had made some radical suggestions, but the group didn't listen and fully consider these ideas. People were thinking for themselves, but nobody was listening. The facilitator reminded us to listen and consider all ideas—even those that may seem crazy at first.

Our next task was more challenging. We were blindfolded and given an eighty-foot rope. Our task was to make a perfect square. All ten participants had to keep both hands on the rope at all times. This time we did a better job of listening. However, we ended up with more of an uneven rectangle than a square.

As the weekend passed, we confronted progressively more challenging assignments. In each exercise there was a key lesson that taught us how to be more creative and how to work more effectively as a team. What is also very obvious now is that our confidence in problem solving increased as we progressed through the various challenges.

The **3-C Leadership Model** helps explain our weekend experience. Each task challenged us in some new way. For example, we had no idea how to get ten people over a fifteen-foot wall. Our confidence level was low. Through brainstorming, experimentation, and coaching from our facilitator, we figured out creative ways to succeed. As we accomplished our goals, we became more confident and eager to take on bigger challenges. We learned how to take our individual skills and incorporate them into a team environment. My key learnings that weekend included:

- Team leaders challenge everyone to think, argue, and debate the issues.

- A team's confidence can grow dramatically when a coach helps people identify and break through the psychological barriers that are holding them back.

- The least amount of coaching (30 seconds or less) often has the most impact.

A Step-Function Change in Results Requires a Step-Function Change in Behavior, Which Requires a Step-Function Change in Thinking.

—sign in the office of Alden Davis, Organizational Change Consultant for the Pratt & Whitney Division of United Technologies, Inc.

CHAPTER 15
Show People What
Good Performance Looks Like

Leaders implement change, which involves new ways of thinking and behaving. An effective coaching technique is showing people what good performance looks like. Being able to see the new behaviors helps people achieve the desired results. For example, in sports you can't expect a player to make the "right moves" if the player doesn't know what the "right moves" are. As one leader puts it, "Telling employees to 'shape up,' 'work hard,' or 'do your best' doesn't send a clear picture of what's expected." (See figure 15.1.)

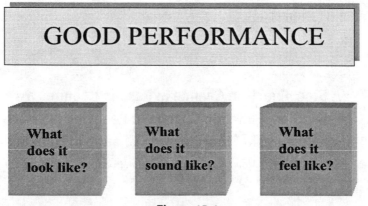

Figure 15.1

SyberVision is a company that subscribes to the "show people what good performance looks like" principle. It trains athletes to improve their skills by watching idealized performances on videotape. For example, athletes who can see the proper stance, grip, and swing of a golf club are more likely to learn and imitate those movements and actions. A management consultant states,

"Expert modeling works for me. You gain the quickest and biggest performance boost by having people watch and learn the skills of the best performers."

If people can see the ideal way to "provide superior customer service," they are better prepared to achieve that goal. Showing people the desired behavior takes the mystery and guesswork out of what's expected. One associate stated, "Seeing how Sue handles customer complaints gave me a clear picture of how a professional operates." Another associate stated, "Having a concrete example to follow reduces stress. Once I had a clear picture, I was able to put all my energy and attention into learning those skills."

When observing examples of top performance, it's best to observe one or two behaviors at a time. For example, when observing effective teamwork, study how the team members resolve conflicts. On another occasion, observe how team members set their agenda and move from one topic to the next.

Top leaders are constantly searching for best practices and outstanding performance in all aspects of business. They encourage others to observe and study people who excel in a particular area. During my career various leaders have said the following to me:

- "Bob runs a terrific meeting. Observe what he does when people don't stick to the agenda."

- "Watch this video of Tom Peters. Study his passion and conviction."

- "Sue's a great team player. You can learn a lot by watching her in team meetings."

Seeing the ideal way to do a task is an excellent first step in any learning or training situation. The next step is practice. Just observing a great golf swing isn't going to make you a great golfer. Practice, along with guidance and feedback from an expert coach, is critical.

Complex tasks need to be broken down into bite-size pieces. People need to see what each piece looks like when it's performed perfectly. For example, a sales presentation might be broken down into precall planning, making introductions and breaking the ice, identifying the buyer's needs, overcoming objections, and closing the sale. Training involves practicing each of these steps and receiving feedback after each practice session. In an article titled "The Myth of Soft-Skills Training," author James C. Georges states that the approach should be to educate briefly, then train at length. This approach is used by sports coaches, martial arts trainers, and coaches in the performing arts. It's a little bit of instruction followed by lots of practice. A management trainer states, "Gaining expertise in any skill requires endless practice. Practice with useful feedback produces continuous improvement."

When effective leader/coaches conduct a practice session, I have observed the following:

- They challenge people to continuously improve on their last performance.

- They show lots of confidence by their words and actions.

- They provide candid and useful feedback that pinpoints how performance can be improved.

Leaders have the attitude "We're never going to stop learning and improving." This attitude causes them to look for best practices and outstanding performances anywhere they go. Seeing is believing and believing makes a task doable.

Conclusion—Show People What Good Performance Looks Like

A director of a hospital wanted his employees to be more "customer focused." In staff meetings and in other employee gatherings, he talked a great deal about the importance of treating patients as customers. However, his comments had little impact in producing any real behavior change. The hospital director decided to try another approach. Several members of his staff and other key contributors were selected to take a weekend cruise aboard one of the top ocean liners. The participants were instructed to observe how they were treated while boarding the ship and throughout their stay. This two-day trip provided many examples of outstanding "customer focus and service." Ship personnel responded quickly to all needs and requests. They frequently used people's names, made eye contact, and showed great care and respect for every passenger. One hospital participant stated, "They made me feel valued and important."

The hospital director showed his staff what great customer service looked like and what it felt like. This experience made a solid and lasting impression on the participants. It started a culture change. Hospital personnel began treating patients like guests on a cruise ship. This is a good example of how "seeing it and experiencing it" makes an abstract concept, like "customer focus," concrete and achievable. It brought life and details to the new behaviors the hospital director was trying to implement.

Leaders practice, then preach — show them first, tell them second.

—sign posted above the desk of a middle manager at a financial services company

CHAPTER 16
Be a Facilitator

Leader/coaches also assist people in planning and implementing change. One way they assist is by performing the role of facilitator. The word "facilitate" means "to make easy." In some situations, individuals and teams need help in following a logical process to achieve their goals. The facilitator supports or makes it easy for the team to fully utilize everyone's ideas, stay on track, and achieve desired outcomes. Phil Beaudoin, leadership consultant and facilitator, states "Good facilitators help the group stick to the agenda, adhere to their operating rules, and follow the steps required for effective planning or problem solving." In this role, the facilitator helps the team become more aware of what they are doing and how they are operating. In essence, the leader is teaching the team that how they make decisions is as important as what they decide.

Like a basketball coach, the facilitator watches the performance of each player individually and the whole team collectively and then offers tips on improvement. In some cases, the facilitator challenges the group by asking questions such as, "What type of performance would be considered best in class?" "If the competition is improving at a rate of 10 percent, should your target be 20 percent?" At other times the facilitator shows confidence and affirms people's skills and creativity: "You were selected to be on this team because of your unique skills and abilities. You are capable of solving this problem." (See figure 16.1.)

The ideal team meeting occurs when people follow the agenda, share information, define problems, and make decisions in a logical, systematic way. Unfortunately, most team meetings don't work that way.

FACILITATOR ROLES

Coach-help the group systematically
follow a process
Challenge-suggest that the group set higher
goals/standards
Confidence-show faith in the group's
ability to succeed

Figure 16.1

Let's consider what happens when a team is trying to define and solve a problem. Since the process involves several steps—

1. Defining the problem,

2. Collecting and analyzing data,

3. Generating alternatives,

4. Evaluating and selecting an alternative, and

5. Implementing—

it's not uncommon to have people attacking the problem from different points of view. For example, one person may be at step 1, trying to define the problem; another at step 3, discussing options; and another at step 5, ready to implement his or her choice. In addition, because most problems require multiple meetings, it's easy to see how people get off track.

Little or no progress is made when everyone is at a different point in the process. Effective facilitators bring the group together. They ask tracking questions, such as "What step are we on?" "What are you trying to do?" "Where are you in the problem-solving process?" Productivity improves as the team works together and systematically goes through each step of the process.

The facilitator must be skillful at knowing when to intervene. Jumping in too soon to help the group can limit team growth. A prime directive for facilitation is this: "Don't do anything for the team that the team members can do for themselves." If you want a team to learn how to work through its own processes, give members a chance to deal with the frustrations, conflicts, and digressions that accompany group communications. When should you intervene? An executive states, "When it's obvious the team is spinning its wheels and getting nowhere, that's the time to intervene and provide assistance."

The facilitator must pay attention to group dynamics. How is the group operating? Is one person dominating the discussion? What messages are being sent by body language? Are people holding back their true feelings? Are some people's ideas being rejected without proper consideration? Are people listening? Who is acting as leader? What's the energy level of the group? What is it the group can't do for itself?

Effective facilitators use a variety of techniques to make sure team members stay on track and fully participate in the discussion:

- **Questioning.** Ask questions to draw people into the discussion, to clarify comments, and to gather information. "Sue, what's your opinion of this option?" "Mike, could you define what you mean by 'best in class'?" "What assumptions have we made in defining the problem?"

- **Probing.** Ask questions that will reveal the feelings behind the facts. "How do you think the customer feels about the delay?" "How do you feel about our mission statement?" "What is your level of commitment to this plan?"

- **Extension.** Ask people to build on the comments made by others. "That's interesting. Could someone add to Joe's comment?" "What would that look like if we were to implement Gina's recommendation?"

- **Focusing and framing.** Make comments or ask questions that keep the group focused on the task at hand. Framing involves putting boundaries or parameters around the topic or problem being discussed. "What problem are we trying to solve?" "Let's consider all options before deciding which is best."

- **Clarifying comments.** Feed back to the speaker your interpretation of his or her comments. This is done to help clarify complex ideas and to make sure ideas are interpreted as intended. "I understand you to be saying that turnover is being caused by the heavy overtime."

- **Linking.** Establish relationships among different ideas. "How does the new testing requirement impact our production schedule?" "How does your recommendation solve the labor problem?"

- **Feedback.** Solicit feedback from the group on what it is accomplishing and how the members are working together. Ask team members to share their views about how the group is working. "Did we meet our objectives?" "Is there commitment to continue this discussion?"

- **Consensus taking.** Ask questions to determine the degree of general agreement among the group. "Does everyone accept this plan?" "Is there opposition to this decision?"

- **Capturing what's said.** Write down key words and comments on a flipchart or whiteboard.

Leader/coaches who perform the role of facilitator help individuals and team members to

- stay focused,

- follow a systematic process, and

- tap into everyone's ideas.

John Nicoletta, consultant and leadership trainer, states, "The best facilitators have a great sense of timing. They understand group dynamics. They know how to draw others into the discussion. And like all great teachers, they help teams become more independent. Eventually, teams can facilitate their own meetings."

Conclusion—Be a Facilitator

I have been a member of over twenty cross-functional teams. These teams were chartered to deal with the topics of improving recruiting practices, reengineering the educational assistance process, identifying best practices in engineering, and applying for the Malcolm Baldrige Award, among others. Most of the teams were made up of eight to ten people. Functions represented included human resources, engineering, information systems, manufacturing, and finance. One of the first tasks each team faced was defining its vision/mission and establishing operating rules. The teams often had a facilitator who helped the members stay on track. In many situations, the facilitator either challenged us, built our confidence, or coached us in how to be more effective. For example, in one team meeting we developed a vision that was less than noteworthy. The facilitator jumped into the discussion and said, "Read it. Is that something that stretches you? Is that vision something you would march behind?" He challenged us to think bigger and strive for a vision that had more impact.

On another occasion, our team did devise a very challenging vision. However, when the group members took a step back and thought about what they had written, there was a sense of "There's no way we are ever going to achieve that vision!" Clearly, our confidence was shaken because of the magnitude of the task. The facilitator reacted and said, "This team has the right people to tackle this problem. Each of you has a unique skill set. You've been successful in the past." He boosted our confidence. He went on to ask, "What small steps can you take toward achieving this vision?" By focusing on small steps, we made progress and gained momentum.

The facilitator also coached us. He intervened with statements such as "Let's stop a moment and look at what's going on here..." or "Let me describe a pattern I've been observing in this meeting." He didn't solve our problems by giving us "the answer." Rather, he forced us to step back and look at what we were doing and why.

Sometimes he privately coached team members after a meeting. Without knowing it, the facilitator was practicing the **3-C Leadership Model**. In essence, he provided the right mix of challenge, confidence building, and coaching.

The creative role of a leader is to facilitate a discussion around what is (current reality) and what could be (vision of the future).

—handwritten note above the desk of an executive at a
large manufacturing company

CHAPTER 17
Give Feedback

Winning leaders set high standards. They believe most people have untapped resources. They willingly give people performance feedback because they know it's needed for improvement. It's also important that feedback is received from multiple sources-customers, peers, team members, and direct reports. One manager states, "My job is to help people reach their potential, perform at their best. In the absence of feedback, people develop an inaccurate perception. We all have improvement opportunities. Both positive feedback and negative feedback are important."

Feedback on the positive side may be even more valuable than negative feedback. Consider a study in which two separate groups tried to improve their bowling skills. In the first group the coach focused on each person's weaknesses and how to correct them. In the second group, the coach pointed out each person's strengths and how to apply their strengths to other aspects of the game. What happened? The first group improved. However, the second group improved more quickly and to a much greater degree. Focusing on people's strengths builds their confidence and determination. However, most experts recommend providing a balance of both positive and negative feedback.

Do leaders always provide negative feedback? A vice president of marketing states, "Providing candid negative feedback is difficult. I struggle every time I have to discuss a person's weaknesses." Some leaders avoid it altogether. Rather than telling someone directly, some managers take the easy way out: They assign poor performers to "special projects," often involving non-value-adding busywork. This is demoralizing and destroys a person's confidence.

Lawrence Bossidy, chairman and CEO of AlliedSignal, states that performance evaluations occur too infrequently, and when they do occur, many leaders act with too much restraint. Doing this not only hurts their companies but also hurts the individuals they are evaluating.

When I was young, the message from many adults was, "If you don't have anything nice to say, don't say anything." That's incorrect. Sometimes the most valuable words to say may not be nice but may be very helpful. What are you really doing when you give negative feedback? First of all, you're challenging people to do better. Second, you're building their confidence by letting them know you believe they can do better. Third, you're coaching them or showing them how to be more effective in the future. Useful feedback includes suggestions for improvement.

Successful leaders are willing to provide "tough love." They're not afraid to tell people change is needed. They don't sugarcoat the message. Their approach could be described as candid and direct. (See figure 17.1.) George David, CEO, says that in a performance culture there must be a willingness to confront change openly, clearly, and with courage. Supervisors must be willing to write a tough performance appraisal if that's what it takes to drive change.

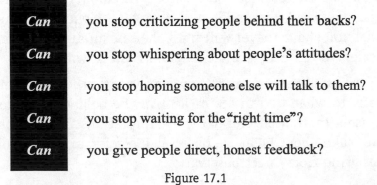

THE FEEDBACK CHALLENGE

Can you stop criticizing people behind their backs?

Can you stop whispering about people's attitudes?

Can you stop hoping someone else will talk to them?

Can you stop waiting for the "right time"?

Can you give people direct, honest feedback?

Figure 17.1

How do you give people negative feedback in a way that affirms your confidence in their abilities? Start the discussion with words like the following:

- "I know you're capable of better performance in the area..."
- "I'm confident you can..."

People willingly consider negative feedback when they know the person giving it believes in them.

Here are some techniques I have found useful when giving people feedback:

- **Ask permission.** Before giving negative feedback, ask permission. The technique is easy. Just ask, "Are you open to some feedback on...?" Naturally, as a manager or leader, you have the authority to *make* employees hear you out. But this doesn't necessarily mean that they will listen. By asking for permission you not only learn whether the time is right, but you also create a bit of curiosity in the mind of the employee. At that point, the stage is set for effective communication.

- **Involve the person.** Ask questions that directly involve people in examining their own performance. "Joe, what's your critique of yesterday's meeting with our field service representatives?" When people diagnose their own performance shortfalls and develop solutions, there's lots of ownership to make it work.

- **Time your discussion.** Generally, the sooner performance problems are discussed, the better. The longer you wait, the less likely the discussion will change behavior. This means that you should never wait until the semiannual performance review to tell people what they did right or wrong.

- **Focus on observations rather than inferences.** Observations refer to what we can see or hear in the behavior of another person. Inferences refer to the interpretations and conclusions we make about what we observe. It's safer to give feedback resulting from direct observations.

- **Keep your emotions in check.** If you correct someone when you're angry, the person will hear the anger and not the content of your message. In many cases, the person may react angrily. Tame your anger before trying to give feedback.

- **Be specific.** Don't make the feedback too general. For example, don't say, "You're not a team player" or "You're not carrying your weight." This kind of feedback doesn't tell the person what specfic behaviors need changing and why.

- **Be realistic.** Rather than making a blanket request for improvement, try telling people what you would like to see *more of* and *less of.* "Jane, I'd like to see you spend less time putting out fires and more time doing strategic planning."

- **Change weaknesses into strengths.** Sometimes a weakness is a strength that's gone too far. For example, someone who has strong interpersonal skills might be too social in the workplace and prevent others from getting their work done. Point out to your employees that with moderation, their weaknesses can be turned into strengths.

- **Offer suggestions for improvement.** The best coaches not only indicate what needs to be done differently, but they also offer their own suggestions on *how* to improve. For example, "Jan, I've pointed out the area needing improvement. Here are three approaches I'd like you to try." Most employees appreciate hearing suggestions on how to be more effective.

- **Be prepared to change.** Learn from the employee's perception of the issue and problem. Be open and prepared to change your own point of view. Being open and willing to change sets a good example for others to follow.

- **End with an affirming statement.** Close your session with a sincere statement that conveys your belief in the person. Let employees know that you have confidence in their ability and determination to improve. "Jack, I'm confident you can improve your performance. You have the skills and abilities to hit the targets we discussed."

- **Follow up.** At the end of your feedback session, ask the person to summarize the main points discussed. What's the action plan? Then jointly set a date for another meeting to check progress.

Leaders believe in people's potential to improve all aspects of their performance. They provide open and honest feedback. But they also hold people accountable for changing and improving their performance. When improvements don't occur, the best leaders are willing to make tough decisions: They fire people who don't support company values or aren't committed to making required changes.

Conclusion—Give Feedback

A former vice president at The Travelers states, "Elizabeth, one of my direct reports, was having difficulty influencing her peers on several reengineering projects. She kept coming to me for help. I coached and encouraged her to try various influencing techniques. However, there was little improvement. She kept reverting to her confrontational style. I finally had to sit down with her and give her some candid, eyeball-to-eyeball performance feedback. However, throughout these tough discussions, Elizabeth knew I had a lot of confidence in her ability to improve. I challenged her to stop relying on her old style of management, which, incidentally, had made her successful in the past. I can't say she made great improvements, but she did improve. Sometimes you have to let go of the old approach before fully commiting to a new approach."

Very often when leaders give feedback, their comments weave in the three variables of challenge, confidence, and coaching. In the above example, the vice president started by challenging Elizabeth to work more effectively with her peers. She showed confidence in Elizabeth's abilities and coached her on influencing techniques. Changing behavior is difficult, especially when a behavior made a person successful in the past. In these situations, many built-in psychological defense mechanisms send people back to their comfort zones. The vice president also gave Elizabeth candid feedback and held her accountable for changing her style.

Ineffective leaders are motivated by the desire to be liked. They don't want to upset anyone. They sugarcoat the negative feedback to the point it becomes sweet. The receiver misses the point. On the other hand, the best leaders aren't worried about being liked. Their focus is helping people reach their potential. Negative and positive feedback are aimed at helping people realize and fully utilize their talents.

Attack the Problem—Not the Person

We will be open and honest with each other and not fear conflict. We will resolve conflict constructively and focus on the process, not the people. We want to be comfortable in giving and receiving feedback and in communicating openly and honestly at all levels.

—one part of the "Code of Champions" used at Rosemount Aerospace

SUMMARY
Coaching to Achieve Top Performance

Below is a list of business leaders and coaches who stepped forward to teach people how to be more effective and successful. Their techniques varied but the common aim was to help people acquire the attitudes, skills, knowledge, and commitment needed to achieve their best performance.

Jesus was a great spritual leader and an outstanding teacher. He taught his followers through stories and parables. Each story had a moral lesson that focused on the proper way to think and behave. He "walked the talk." He was a positive role model who exemplified ethical and moral behavior.

Socrates, the Greek philosopher, spent the greater part of his mature life in the marketplace and public resorts of Athens in dialogue and argument with anyone who would listen. His basic method of teaching was asking questions. His questions and interrogations probed issues and forced people to engage in self-examination. Asking the right questions is often much more powerful than simply providing the right answer.

Debbie Fields, CEO and president of Mrs. Field's Cookies, constantly coaches people. She says that people don't always like what she has to say, but part of her job is to specifically identify what people could be doing better.

Don Shula, former NFL coach of the Miami Dolphins, said that he made sure his players came out of every meeting a little more intelligent. After every practice his players were better prepared to play, both mentally and physically. He set high expectations and challenged all of his players to reach their potential.

Pat Summitt, head coach of the University of Tennessee's women's basketball team, selects, trains, and motivates her players to excel. Four of her teams won NCAA Division One titles. In 1984, Pat coached the women's Olympic basketball team that won a gold medal. One of her key beliefs is that she must challenge players to expand on their talent and on their views of what they're capable of achieving.

Mahatma Gandhi is considered to be a great spiritual and political leader. He taught and coached his followers mainly by setting the example. Gandhi promoted nonviolent civil disobedience as the most appropriate method for achieving political and social goals. His courage and conviction were demonstrated numerous times. For example, he was jailed for a total of seven years for various civil disobedience activities.

Jamie Escalante was an outstanding high school math teacher. He was featured in the 1988 film *Stand and Deliver*. His unique and demanding style helped his students excel. He showed great confidence in his students and frequently asked them to believe in themselves, be disciplined, and work hard. For the first ten weeks of class he didn't use a book. Rather, he did experiments in class to point out various applications of calculus.

Dr. W. Edwards Deming was an outstanding teacher and coach. He taught people how to use and apply statistics to improve quality in business and industry. Deming used simple stories, examples, and experiments to explain concepts and teach his philosophy. His basic philosophy was that quality improves as variability decreases. Finally, he demonstrated unwavering commitment. He would simply stop working with clients who didn't demonstrate a total commitment to quality.

General Norman Schwartzkopf was the U.S. Commander of the Allied forces during the Gulf War. One of his practices and principles of commanding a division involved teaching and coaching. He believed that all commanders had the responsibility to teach and train their subordinates just as they had been mentored by others.

All of these leaders used a variety of techniques to coach and teach people. Each leader was a positive role model who "practiced what he/she preached." A common theme is that each coach was demanding and didn't settle for a second-rate performance. These leaders not only built up people's knowledge and skills, they also strengthened people's confidence and self-esteem. They helped people achieve their best performance.

Case Study—Applying the 3-C Leadership Model

Chapters 13–17 described several ways leaders coach, teach, and mentor people. The following case studies highlight how Jay Goltz and Jim Ligotti have applied the **3-C Leadership Model**. Jay is president of Artist's Frame Service, and Jim is global product manager for Carrier Corporation.

Case Study—Applying the 3-C Leadership Model

To be a great company, you have to apply all 3 Cs (challenge, build confidence, and coach). Some leaders employ one C and their companies never reach their full potential. Lots of average companies settle for a 5 percent return. Great companies have these attributes:

1. Customers who are more than satisfied, they're thrilled. They love your service and products.

2. Employees who are passionate about their jobs. They feel connected to the business. They are constantly learning, growing, and developing.

3. Profit. Great companies have a good bottom line.

I challenge people to be the best they can be. Consistent best performance is the key. If it takes three hours to do a task, I'll ask, "Can we do it in two hours?" Last week at a meeting with my production managers I said, "We did well this year but we can do better." I also challenge my managers to give people candid feedback. Being able and willing to handle confrontation is important. You can't keep people in your organization about whom you would say, if they resigned, "Great, thank God." I have 125 great employees because I fired many people along the way who had bad attitudes.

Self-confidence is a trait people need to take risks and make quick decisions. Fear often holds people back. One of my favorite questions is, "What's the worst that can happen?" Getting clear about the worst outcome helps put everything in perspective. I also believe in giving people the tools they need to succeed. If you're going to be the best at anything, you can't be afraid of making mistakes. Leaders need to have the resolve and determination that they are going to run a great company. That means having confidence in themselves and in their employees, and not settling for anything less than excellent results.

Achieving greatness almost always requires a coach or teacher to help you along the way. In the retail industry, coaching often involves helping people have the right attitude or viewpoints. In my experience, day-to-day events can sometimes make people forget or drift away from our business beliefs and principles. For example, when an employee says to a customer, "I'll see what I can do," that's not the right attitude. That's not going to make us a great company. We don't tolerate any attitudes less than "We'll do anything we reasonably can to satisfy the customer." Setting the example is also an aspect of coaching. If I don't practice what I preach, who's going to follow?

The best leaders not only challenge people but also coach them on how to succeed. Different people require different Cs. However, people's needs do change. On one task a person might need a confidence boost. At another time the same person might need a challenge to motivate him or her to perform at a higher level. What I have learned is that if a person needs all 3 Cs at the same time, that person probably is in the wrong position.

—Jay Gotz
President
Artist's Frame Service

▲

Case Study—Applying the 3-C Leadership Model

A lot of my job involves managing projects and leading people to find new and better ways of meeting tough challenges. I view myself as a coach. I try to build people's confidence and challenge them to think and take action.

To achieve anything significant, people need confidence. To build people's confidence I like to start by having a conversation about their non-work-related activities. My objective is to find out their interests and in what areas they have excelled or achieved some particular success. It might be a sport, hobby, or a social activity. I find everyone has achieved success in some aspect of his or her life. I also try to focus on what people did to achieve success. When people talk about where they've been and what they achieved, that's a confidence boost. The more I can relate to people in their world, the more effective I can be. Then I bring the discussion back to business. I often ask people to describe where they are now on a project and where they want to get to. What's the desired outcome? It's critical there's agreement on the vision, the desired future state. There are always problems and obstacles that separate current reality versus where you want to be. What squashes many people's initiative are the instantaneous objections that define why something can't be done. When challenges seem overwhelming or when people are reluctant to change, I go back to their success in the non-work-related areas. I remind people what they did to achieve success in other areas of their life. This helps people see the business challenge in a new context.

Once people believe they can succeed, it's a matter of coaching them in how to make it happen. Coaching involves helping people clearly see the obstacles. It's almost like the sales process. What are the objections and how can they be overcome? Very often I find that the obstacles people identify aren't the real problem. They're symptoms of some other deeper issue that's holding the person back. It's very important to peel back the onion and identify the root-cause problem. In doing this, leaders need to be sensitive. What might seem like a minor problem to me might be viewed as a serious issue to the person. You never want to embarrass the person. I ask open-ended questions. I want people to work through their problems and I also want them to develop their own recommendations. The more that happens, the more confident people become.

My role as a leader is to coach people. However, before I can be an effective coach, people need to trust that I know where I'm going. They also need to understand my vision and philosophy of how to win in the marketplace. The 3 C Leadership Model has helped me realize I need to balance my efforts in the three areas of coaching, challenging, and building confidence. The best leaders help people remove actual and sometimes imagined barriers and obstacles.

—Jim Ligotti

Global Product Manager
Carrier Corporation

PART V
Setting the Example

Leadership is really about helping people change. However, before you can influence others to change, you must set the example. I like to periodically remind myself of the following:

- Before I can challenge other people, I must challenge myself.

- Before I can build someone else's self-confidence, I must develop my own confidence.

- Before I can teach others, I must first learn the new skill or technique.

When leaders set the example, they gain credibility. Tricia Day, chief labor relations officer for the Massachusetts Bay Transportation Authority (MBTA), states, "I challenge myself by always setting high standards and accepting additional responsibilities. Setting high standards forces me to go the extra mile in terms of doing my homework, being prepared, and being professional in all dealings with managers and union officials. In all areas of my job, if I don't set the example, I don't have credibility when I try to influence behaviors or implement practices."

Conversely, when leaders don't set the example, or when they say one thing and do another, their credibility is destroyed. Even small disparities between words and actions create distrust. Without credibility it's nearly impossible to influence others to follow. A characteristic of all great leaders is that what they think, say, and do are all the same. This consistency makes them very credible. Another aspect of credibility is staying well informed and up-to-date. Effective leaders keep up with the latest information, ideas, and trends. They pay attention to the marketplace. People will not put their trust and faith in a person who they feel is two years behind the times.

In addition to setting the example and being credible, leaders must find the desire to step forward and take on a leadership role. The best leaders have a burning desire to make a difference. They believe in themselves and their abilities to diagnose what other people need to succeed. Finally, leaders must have excellent communication and influencing skills. They must be able to clearly and succinctly explain their ideas, tell their stories, and convince others to take action. In addition, leaders need good listening skills to understand people's concerns, ideas, and goals.

Chapter 18 explains the actions you need to take to first lead yourself and then to lead others. (See figure V-1.) Chapter 19 describes how three senior managers have implemented the **3-C Leadership Model**.

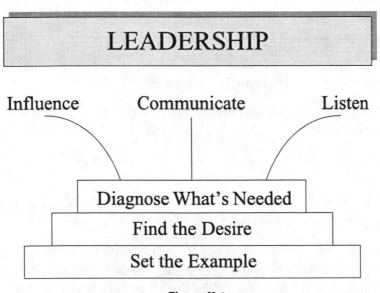

Figure V-1

CHAPTER 18
Lead Yourself and Others

Before you can lead others, you have to learn how to lead yourself. You must set the example. According to the **3-C Leadership Model**, that means you must challenge yourself, build your confidence, and continuously learn new skills and strategies.

Challenge Yourself

You have to stretch yourself and push beyond your comfort zone. If you never take risks, what type of message does that send? Consider challenging yourself by doing some of the following:

- Try one new approach to running a meeting, making a presentation, or giving people feedback.

- Visit other companies, and identify one new approach you will try back on your job.

- Take a course and learn a new skill that's outside your area of expertise.

- Volunteer to be part of a project team that's dealing with a tough community issue.

A former assistant treasurer of a Fortune 500 company states, "I force myself to get involved in new and challenging activities away from the office. If I can't take risks and show I'm capable of changing, how can I expect my direct reports to change?" The good news is that the farther you get out of your comfort zone, the more you will be noticed. When senior managers look for promotional candidates, you will make the list.

Build Your Confidence

Leaders need confidence in their own skills and abilities. A common characteristic of top executives and leaders is they believe in themselves. As one of my mentors stated, "If you don't have confidence in your own words and message, who will?" Self-confidence also helps leaders be candid communicators. They don't sugarcoat the message. Confident leaders are willing to ask others for help and guidance. People who lack confidence are often afraid to ask for the very advice that could help them be more effective.

Get in touch with your inner skills and talents. Build on your positive accomplishments. One of my colleagues recommends, "Keep a vivid mental picture of yourself when you were at your best, not at your worst." Let go of your negative thoughts and fears. We all have had bad experiences, but some people keep repeating them. Successful people learn from failure.

A former vice president of The Travelers told me the following: "I've learned there are two parts to self-confidence. One has to do with being prepared, doing my homework, and having up-to-date skills. The other part is more spiritual. It's believing and following your inner voice, not doubting your conscience."

Be A Student

Ongoing education, training, and development of yourself is the third area in which you must set the example. Before you can be a good coach and mentor, you must learn how to be a good student. Tricia Day states, "Being a good student and an effective teacher are two sides of the same coin. I try to learn and gain new insights each time I perform either role." Good students can discern what they need to know, how they learn most effectively, and how to apply what they learn. Being a good student also requires you to develop

- organizational skills,
- listening skills,
- knowledge of your strengths and weaknesses,

- an understanding of how to utilize performance feedback, and
- the ability to be an effective team player.

In turn, these skills help you become an effective teacher and coach. Noel Tichy and Eli Cohen, in their book *The Leadership Engine*, state that one of the factors that makes leaders such great teachers is that they are great students. Every day there are lessons to be learned. Leaders are proficient at recognizing those lessons and using them to prosper.

By challenging yourself, building your self-confidence, and being a student, you are setting the example and gaining the credibility needed to lead others. Living by his or her word is a leader's most powerful tool. People instantly lose credibility when they say one thing and do the opposite.

Leading Others

Some people achieve great credibility but have difficulty leading others. To lead others, not only must you set the example, but you must also inspire others to succeed. A program director states, "The basis of leadership is the capacity of the leader to influence the attitudes, beliefs, and behaviors of other people. Convincing people there's something bigger and better." Some of the additional traits and skills needed to lead others are the following:

- **Desire**—a willingness and desire to lead.
- **Diagnostic Skills**—an ability to listen, observe, and discern where people need help. What is it they can't do for themselves?
- **Influencing Skills**—an ability to connect with people in such a way that they become receptive to new ideas and new options.
- **Communication Skills**—an ability to convey ideas and information that are clear, concise, and complete.
- **Listening Skills**—an ability to hear, interpret, and evaluate another speaker's words and body language.

Gandhi's message:
Become the change you seek.
—sign above the desk of an executive at a large insurance company

Desire to Lead

Leaders want to lead. Leadership is all about trying to influence one or more people to follow your direction. In every situation there is a relationship between the potential leader and the potential follower. The potential follower enters the relationship with desires and needs (known or unknown). The potential leader enters the relationship with ideas and suggestions to help the follower.

Every time a leader enters a relationship, there is a possibility of rejection. The follower can say, in effect, "No, that's not the problem" or "I don't agree with the direction you're taking." People who aren't willing to take a risk never try to influence others. On the other hand, if you have a desire to lead, you're willing to enter the zone of uncertainty. As one of my colleagues stated, "You must have desire and courage to be a leader. If you fear rejection or are overly concerned with 'What will people think?' you'll never succeed as a leader." The key to making the mental leap to "demanding excellence" is to overcome your fear of failure or rejection.

In a management seminar that involved the topic "facing your fears," a participant told the following story: "I was in a strategic planning meeting with fifteen people representing all functional groups. As the plan took shape, I had serious doubts. It was too ordinary. It occurred to me to say something, but I paused, fearing rejection. The moment for action passed and I sat silently, saying nothing." When people don't speak up or take action, others lose the benefits of their insights and ideas. Missed opportunities are gone forever.

Leadership requires you to take risks and do tasks others are not willing to do, including making unpopular decisions. Try answering these questions:

1. Do you have a desire to lead? When? In what situations?

2. Do you fear rejection? When? In what situations?

3. Do you believe the company needs you and depends on your leadership?

4. To what extent do you want to help people reach or exceed their potential?

The vice president of sales and marketing of a consumer electronics products company was asked, "What people make the best salespeople?" He walked up to the flipchart and on the left side listed a number of qualities—communication skills, good track record, background in electronics, and product knowledge. On the right side of the chart he wrote this: "Fire in the heart." Passion, fire, desire—these are the qualities that will take you from average to outstanding. These are also the qualities that people need to be leaders.

Where do desire, and passion come from? I've asked that question of several leaders. These are some of their responses:

- "Our vision made me passionate. I strongly believed in what we were doing."

- "Somewhere along the way I learned it was very exciting and rewarding to help other people achieve their dreams. That's what leaders do."

- "My desire comes from the fact I believe my company will be better if I take a leadership role. Maybe that's arrogant, but it motivates me."

- "I'm a high achiever. Pursuing excellence is exciting because it separates me from the crowd."

Leaders want to make a difference. They're willing to take risks, overcome their fears, and make it known what they believe. Leaders have the desire to make the difference.

Leadership springs from deep personal conviction.

—Peter Senge

The following case study describes how Charlie Eitel, president and chief operating officer of Interface, Inc., developed his leadership skills.

▲

Case Study—The Desire to Lead

When I was in elementary school, my classmates almost always nominated me for homeroom president. This amazed me because back then I was not an academic leader. For some reason people thought I had leadership skills. At that early age it never dawned on me what was really happening. Now I realize how few people truly want to lead others. To want to be the leader is to risk failure. I'm convinced that everyone is afraid to fail—it's all a matter of degree. Fear is what causes most people to "play not to lose."

But when we "play not to lose," we don't take chances, we avoid pain, we stay in our comfort zones. On the other hand, "playing to win" is about taking risks, stretching ourselves, pursuing our dreams. Early in life I decided I wanted to play to win. It's more exciting. There is a great deal of self-satisfaction in helping others pursue their dreams and goals. I don't want to find myself in a nursing home someday thinking that all I did was play it safe. My passion is to discover what's possible. My grandfather said that love and money are the only reasons why people do something they would not do naturally. I love to lead.

—Charlie Eitel

President and COO
Interface, Inc.

Diagnostic Skills

Leaders need to be able to diagnose situations to determine exactly what individuals or teams need. In essence, leaders ask, "What problem can't they solve? What's holding them back?" By listening to what people say and observing what they do, leaders begin to get clues as to what leadership action (challenge, confidence, coaching) is needed. A senior executive stated, "You need to stop thinking about yourself and start focusing on what others are going through. What are their needs? This is the opposite way of thinking for most people. To lead other people you must know what others are thinking and feeling."

As you listen to what the individuals or teams are saying, comments like the following may indicate a need for a tougher challenge:

- "We're getting good results; let's not worry about next year."
- "I don't think we should change. Let's keep doing what worked in the past."
- "I'm content just to do my job and retire in five years."
- "Don't mess things up. Just leave well enough alone."

Comments like the following may demonstrate a need for building confidence:

- "How can we compete with a company twice our size?"
- "There's no way we can do this any faster (or make it cheaper or improve quality)."
- "We need to do several more studies (or bring in consultants or benchmark)." (Delay tactics may indicate a lack of confidence.)

Comments like the following indicate a need for coaching:

- "We're not sure of our priorities. What should be our next step?"
- "What problem are we trying to solve?"
- "How should we reengineer this process?"
- "We haven't sold to a large retail chain for a long time."

Certainly, as you listen to individuals and teams, you hear a variety of comments. Identify the common themes. What are the recurring messages the individuals are saying about themselves and their peers? Also, take note of their body language.

In addition, observing individuals and teams in a variety of settings is helpful. How do people behave? Who sets the agenda? Are there inconsistencies in what people say and do? Is progress being made? The following are additional questions to consider:

Challenge: Are challenging goals established? Do people question and challenge each other's ideas? What's the energy level and motivation of the group?

Confidence: Do people willingly state their points of view? What does nonverbal behavior, such as posture and eye contact, indicate about confidence? Do people aggressively tackle problems?

Coaching: How effectively do people communicate? What approach is used to dissect and analyze problems? How are decisions made? How are conflicts resolved? Does the group follow an orderly process?

The objective of listening to and observing people is to identify their patterns of thinking and behaving. This information determines the type of leadership action (challenge, confidence, coaching) that is needed. Leaders make it a habit to observe and listen to people on a regular basis. In every meeting and one-on-one interaction there are new insights to gain.

Leadership is a reciprocal process between those who choose to lead and those who choose to follow. Any discussion of leadership must attend to the dynamics of this process.

—Jim Kouzes and Barry Posner

The following case study describes how Frank Maguire, president of Health Communications Group, uses listening techniques to reinforce his leadership skills.

▲

Case Study—Diagnosing What's Needed

I always try to be aware of what's going on around me. That means observing people, not once or twice, but all the time. It also means listening. Within the word "listen" there is another word—"silent." Remaining silent and really listening to people's point of view is critical. Leaders need to look from a floodlight, big picture point of view. The more I observe and listen, the more I understand where people want to go and what's holding them back.

Management is a cognitive, linear process; leadership is an art that has a spiritual quality. An essential part of leadership is invisible—what is on the inside of a manager. I have to diagnose what my inner voice is telling me. I can't be an effective leader if I'm unclear about my primary values and beliefs. Being quiet and listening to yourself on a regular basis is very important.

The bottom line is that leaders must first diagnose themselves and get in touch with their personal mission and vision. Next, they diagnose the people around them. After making the proper diagnoses, leaders institute the necessary actions that help others grow, learn, develop, and ultimately reach the desired potential.

—Frank Maguire

President
Health Communications Group

Influencing Skills

Along with credibility, leaders must be able to package their message so it influences people to follow. My mother, who was a sales representative for a school supply company, used to tell me, "The most important skill needed in business is 'selling.' Nothing much happens until someone sells a product or idea." Leaders are selling ideas and trying to influence people all the time. They're selling their vision, their belief in people, and their coaching techniques. Successful leaders connect with people in a way that makes them receptive to considering new ideas. One executive states, "To influence people, the challenge is to make others see the advantage to themselves in responding to your idea or proposal."

One way not to influence people is to argue with them. No matter how right you are, no matter how wrong the other person might be, you will never get them to consider new ideas by putting them on the defensive. My colleague, Tony Borgen, states, "When people get defensive they close down. It's emotional. They stop listening." Influential leadership is more about opening people up to new ideas and possibilities.

According to Jay Conger, professor of organizational behavior at the University of Southern California, the most effective persuaders are open-minded. They are willing to adjust their positions and incorporate other ideas. A program manager states, "Ironically, it is our willingness to listen and understand others first that gives us the power to persuade people to accept our position." In addition, Conger makes the point that effective persuaders use stories, metaphors, and analogies along with numerical data to make their positions come alive.

Stories are particularly effective because they touch people's emotions and their intellect. Leadership author and trainer Tom Peters uses stories almost exclusively in conducting his seminars. His stories influence participants to rethink their business strategies. Stories are also effective because they point out how an individual or team dealt with a tough challenge and achieved success. You can influence people in a number of ways.

- **First, sell yourself.** Do your homework. Be prepared. Be current on your topic. Leadership consultant, Phil Beaudoin states, "The first impression you make is important. Look professional. The way you dress, your posture, body language and enthusiasm –all send big messages to your audience." Remember leaders are always onstage, being watched and observed.

- **Provide simple logic.** Explain the key reasons why people should follow your direction. The first reason you present should be the strongest, most compelling one. Effective persuaders follow the **KISS** formula—**k**eep **i**t **s**imple and **s**uccinct. Use simple explanations, and examples to make your case.

- **Having a Strong Point of View.** Leaders need to present their ideas without any hesitation or waffling. There's no room for tentativeness when you're challenging people or confirming confidence in their abilities. If people sense any doubt in your conviction, then your ability to influence is lost. Michael Eisner, CEO of Walt Disney, says that it's always the person with a strong point of view who influences the group. What often separates leaders from the pack is the depth of their conviction.

- **Selling the Benefits.** People want to know: What's in it for me? Selling the benefits means explaining how the new change will help people be more successful. A vice president states, "Don't assume the benefits are obvious. People don't always make the connections." Successful leaders often sell the benefits at two levels. First, they describe the win for the individual. Second, they make it clear how the change will help the business unit or company. Leadership consultant, John Nicoletta states, "Some leaders make the mistake of only talking about the features of a new program. When you discuss benefits you connect with what's meaningful to the individual."

- **Presenting Testimonials.** Another way leaders influence people is by pointing out what other respected people have said about a particular idea or strategy. For example, in trying to influence a group of people to adopt a six sigma quality program, I might quote what a leading CEO has said about the benefits of six sigma quality. (The objective of six sigma quality is to achieve virtually error-free performance in products and services.) The president of a small ice cream company states, "I've been influenced several times to consider new products simply because someone I respected said that it worked for them. People endorse what they believe in." Endorsements are most effective if they come from people who are credible.

Leaders realize that influencing people is not a one-time event. It's an ongoing process. It often takes many tries before you get people's acceptance and commitment. Leaders don't give up. They keep refining their message and delivery. When you're passionate about your beliefs, you find a way to convince others to follow.

Behind every open door needs to be an open mind.

—sign above the door of a director of information systems

The following case study describes how Tricia Day, chief labor relations officer of the Massachusetts Bay Transportation Authority, uses influencing skills.

▲

Case Study—Influencing Skills

Before trying to influence someone, I try to first understand his or her point of view and needs. What I've found is people aren't open to my suggestions if they don't think I understand their situation. Another way I influence people is by pointing out solutions or approaches that have solved similar problems. One of my previous bosses said, "If you pay attention to the details, you gain credibility. Then, when the bigger strategic issues are being discussed, people will listen to your ideas."

I've also learned to be a good listener. It's more than just listening to the words; it's a matter of reading between the lines. Very often what I'm being told isn't the real issue. Being able to prod and cross-examine in a way that doesn't put the person on the defensive is important.

Another important part of effective communications is being direct and straightforward. Leaders can't avoid issues or be indecisive. I believe in being clear, direct, and to the point in all communications. Having confidence in yourself and your beliefs provides the energy to be forceful and direct.

—Tricia Day

Chief Labor Relations Officer
Massachusetts Bay Transportation Authority

Communication Skills: Sending Information

What's different about the way effective leaders communicate? Research by Professor Roderick Hart of the University of Texas indicates that leaders frequently use words that can be categorized as

- realistic (candid, direct, no spin, positive or negative),

- optimistic (upbeat and positive),

- action-oriented (goals, deadlines, results), or

- certain (decisive, no waffling).

Leaders package their message with the right balance of realism and optimism. They describe what is and what could be. They generate a sense of urgency about pursuing and achieving important goals. Their words create excitement and action. In addition, they communicate their ideas with certainty. They project confidence in that they know where they are going and how to get there.

Leaders use many of the following communication techniques:

1. Connect the Dots. People want to know how the present challenge or new initiative relates to the big picture. How do all the pieces fit together? Effective leaders connect the dots with statements like "Let me tell you how this new improvement initiative relates to our overall strategy" or "Let me give you some background information and explain how this relates to our quality program."

2. Provide Dramatic Contrast. When leaders describe situations, problems, and opportunities, they often provide a dramatic contrast between good and bad, right and wrong, changing and not changing. By contrasting, the leader simplifies the issues and helps followers clearly understand what must be done and why.

3. Motivate the Listener. Followers want to know, if we achieve a stretch goal, what do we receive? Leaders often start by explaining how people will benefit from what is being proposed. They clearly answer the question, What's in it for the listener?" Another way leaders motivate people to pay attention is by using signal words. For example:

- "Listen carefully to these instructions."
- "Pay attention to this; change is needed."
- "If you don't remember anything else, remember this."

These types of statements tell the audience to pay attention and listen.

4. Follow Abstract Concepts with Concrete Examples. Abstract concepts, such as "customer focus" and "teamwork," can be interpreted in many ways. Effective leaders follow abstract concepts with concrete examples so that listeners will have a solid understanding of what's meant. Examples and illustrations provide tangible reference points to make the point.

5. Use Precise Words. Effective leaders use precise words, such as "12 percent increase" or "10 a.m. on Tuesday." Words like "large increase" or "as soon as possible" are vague and can be interpreted in many ways. Using precise words reduces the chances of communication breakdowns. As mentioned above, research has shown that leaders commonly use words connoting certainty, such as "We will . . ." or "It's a fact that . . ." Using precise words also indicates that the leader is decisive.

6. Create a Visual Picture. A visual picture lets the receiver clearly see what is being described. For example, "The red BMW convertible" is easy to visualize. Describing a visual picture that is vital, compelling, and energizing helps followers see where they are going and how the future will be better.

7. Keep It Simple. Effective leaders have the ability to keep their message simple. Simple messages have impact and are easy to remember. The best communicators use simple stories, examples, and illustrations to make their points.

8. Keep It Short. George David, CEO of United Technologies, Inc., speaking to a group of graduate business students at Yale University, stated that clarity and brevity are critical. You cannot make your message short enough. I believe some of the most influential leadership messages come in three-word phrases. (See figure 18.1.)

LEADERSHIP MESSAGES

Challenge	Confidence	Coaching
"Raise your standards."	"You're the best."	"Benchmark the best."
"Select the best."	"Drive out fear."	"Learning is lifelong."
"Just say no."	"We're number one."	"Do it now."

Figure 18.1

9. Tell Stories. Leaders tell stories. Stories hold people's interest and are an effective way to describe a challenge and the steps taken to achieve success. The best stories are personal. They describe how a leader faced difficulty, personally struggled, experienced doubt, and found a way to succeed.

In summary, leaders develop excellent communication skills. Their message is clear and focused. Their delivery is powerful and persuasive.

Communication is the translator between vision and results.

—sign on the office wall of Susan W. Lewis, Executive Vice President,
The Travelers Realty Investment Company

The following case study lists and describes how Michael Z. Kay, president and chief executive officer of LSG Sky Chefs, Inc., communicates with his employees.

Case Study—Communication Skills

Our company went through a major turnaround between 1992 and 1995. Our biggest problems were operational. We were the industry laggard in terms of productivity, costs, and profits. We had to communicate our problems in ways that broke through people's defenses, rationalizations, and excuses. The talent and abilities within all levels of management had to be unlocked. My advice for effective communications includes the following:

- Before you start to communicate, condense your message into one to three simple business initiatives. A new program every month won't work. Repeat your messages over and over, and state your message with passion, enthusiasm, and conviction.

- Create monumental goals. Stretch people out of their comfort zones. Nothing commands people's attention like demanding targets and timetables.

- Provide people with new skills and new tools. This communicates your commitment to helping people climb the mountain and reach the top.

- Let people know you believe in them. You can always find know-how, insight, and even managerial brilliance within the business.

- Give frequent, candid feedback. Let people know where they are strong but also where they need to improve. Always demonstrate your confidence in people's ability to learn and grow.

- Establish rigorous consequences. This does not mean penalties for not achieving stretch goals, but the consequences of not changing the way you work. There is an important distinction.

- Set the example. In any turnaround or major change, all eyes are on the leader. If the leader doesn't demonstrate total commitment to the new values and practices, why should anyone else?

- Celebrate success. Shine the spotlight on every win—small or large.

Leaders communicate in many ways—in what they say, what they measure, even in what they celebrate. Being aligned and consistent in each area is important. Having a clear, simple message that's stated with passion and conviction is vital.

—Michael Z. Kay

President and CEO
LSG Sky Chefs, Inc.

Listening Skills: Receiving Information

Leaders spend a lot of time communicating their vision, values, and key initiatives. Equally important, they must spend time listening to customers, suppliers, and employees from all parts of the organization. Over the past ten years I've asked many people, "How do you feel when people truly listen to your ideas?" Answers have included: "valued," "respected," "that my opinion was worthwhile," and "I was part of a team." Leaders who are effective listeners not only discover numerous good ideas, but also make people feel valued and respected.

Some leaders falsely think that the more they talk, the more they lead. Often, the reverse is true: The more you listen and ask probing questions, the more effective you are as a leader. Smart leaders know that the person asking the questions determines the agenda. Leaders are motivated to listen. They are very curious and want to know what people think and why. Dr. Mitchell Rabkin, CEO of Beth Israel Hospital in Boston, has a small figurine of a little boy on his desk. The child is squatting, picking up something, and looking it over. Dr. Rabkin says that the statue is there to remind people of how important it is for everyone to be curious with no preconceptions. Asking questions, listening, and learning are important activities for every leader.

The following techniques support effective listening:

1. Make the Time. In your own behavior make listening and fully understanding others as important as speaking and presenting your ideas. Make listening a priority.

2. Face the Speaker Squarely. Making eye contact is important because it helps form a bond between speaker and listener. Facing the speaker gives a leader a chance to observe body language. Certainly, the spoken words are important, but tone of voice and body language also convey important information. For example, a lot can be learned about a person's confidence level by observing these two factors.

3. Listen at Two Levels. One level of listening involves what the words mean. A deeper level of listening has to do with what's behind the words. For exmple, if an associate said, "Don't bother going to the quarterly review meeting," the words are clear. The feelings behind the words may be the real message. Ask questions and probe to find out the underlying feelings. Leaders need to understand people's gut-level feelings before they can decide how to respond.

4. Require Vague Terms to Be Defined. Many words are ambiguous and can be interpreted in different ways. To reduce the possibility of communication breakdowns, effective listeners require vague terms be defined. For example, if the speaker uses the term "excellence" or "outstanding," the listener might ask, "How do you define excellence?" or "What do you mean by 'outstanding'?"

5. When Attention Wanders, Use Focus Words. When a leader doesn't pay attention or listen effectively, the speaker concludes that the leader doesn't care. Listening is hard work and one's attention can wander at times. When your attention wanders, say focus words to yourself, such as "Tune in," "Concentrate," or "Stop and focus." These reminders help you stay in the present moment and listen.

6. Ask Questions. As needed, ask questions to obtain more information or to clarify what the speaker has said. It's best to ask one question at a time and then listen carefully to the reply. Follow-up questions are usually necessary to identify underlying assumptions and feelings.

7. Listen to the Pain. When you receive bad news, don't shoot the messenger. As a matter of fact, you should welcome bad news with open arms. Seek understanding. Validate what you see and hear. Bad news is really a gift. It gives you a chance to identify problems and take corrective action. (See figure 18.2.)

8. Listen for What Is Not Being Said. Sometimes what's most significant is the topic the speaker is avoiding. Leaders need to create an open environment and invite discussion on the difficult topics.

CONFIDENCE AND LISTENING

Being confident with yourself protects you from

- becoming defensive or vague
- avoiding difficult topics
- personalizing disagreements
- feeling down because someone else has a better idea

Figure 18.2

When asked, "What would you do differently?" many former presidents and CEOs say they would spend more time listening to employees, customers, and suppliers. What's on their mind? What are their ideas, problems, and concerns? This feedback provides important information from several points of view.

Leaders know the importance of having effective communication skills both in sending and receiving information. Effective leaders frequently ask others for feedback on their message and communication skills. "How did people react to my speech?" "Did people feel their concerns were heard?" "How could I have more effectively handled the question on overtime?" Leaders constantly fine-tune their message and the techniques they use to communicate.

The following case study demonstrates how Dr. Tony Allessandra, author of *Charisma* and *The Platinum Rule,* developed the listening skills required of leaders who want to motivate their employees.

▲

Case Study—Listening Skills and Motivation

Effective listening makes me a better leader. For one thing, people feel valued and appreciated when you truly listen to their ideas. I try to create a positive listening environment. When a person speaks, I try to put the person at ease by creating a relaxed, accepting environment. I never want to give the impression that I want to jump right in and start talking. It's always important to stay in the present and focus on the speaker.

I treat every conversation as an opportunity to gain that one piece of information that will give me the edge. The edge in terms of understanding people, connecting with them, and being able to lead them in more effective ways. I talk with lots of people—presidents of companies, senior managers, customers, suppliers, and employees throughout the company. Each person has a piece of the puzzle that helps me see the complete picture. Focused listening helps me gain a deeper insight into what people are thinking and feeling. My motto is—Look for that something special you can learn from each and every person you meet. Great leaders effectively use personal power which has a strong connection to the ability to listen to what people say, as well as how they say it.

Being a good listener also means being comfortable with silence. A few seconds of dead air are OK. Sometimes the best information is stated after a brief period of silence. Gut level feelings, including bad news, are important to hear. I want people to be candid and let me know what they are really feeling. Leaders have the self-confidence needed to stay open and not become defensive.

The rules of good listening include all of the techniques such as making eye contact, asking questions, and observing body language. However, a very key part of listening is also the desire or motivation to learn what people are thinking. It is difficult, if not impossible, to lead people without first understanding where people are now and where they want to go.

—Dr. Tony Alessandra

Keynote Speaker and Author of *Charisma* and *The Platinum Rule*
www.alessandra.com

Conclusion—Lead Yourself and Others

Before you can lead others you must lead yourself. That involves challenging yourself, building your self-confidence, and being committed to ongoing education and training. When you set the example you gain instant credibility.

In addition to setting the example, leaders must possess desire and skills as follows:

- *Desire*—a strong willingness to help people grow and develop. Desire and courage to make a difference, to take risks, and challenge the status quo.

- *Diagnostic Skills*—an ability to quickly figure out what's needed and why.

- *Influencing Skills*—an ability to convince others to follow your lead.

- *Communication Skills*—an ability to clearly and succinctly state your ideas and feelings.

- *Listening Skills*—an ability to fully understand other people's thoughts and feelings.

Good interpersonal skills are important because they make the connection between leader and follower. The best leaders are often described with comments such as "excellent communicator," "good listener," "convincingly sells his ideas," "takes the time to hear you out," and "good at problem solving and resolving conflicts."

Go beyond asking questions. Be curious with no preconceptions. Keep a beginner's mind.

— sign on the desk of a vice president of operations at a small consulting company

CHAPTER 19
Applying the 3-C Leadership Model

The **3-C Leadership Model** provides a specific, integrated road map leaders can follow to help people become more and achieve more than they ever thought possible. Figure 19.1 provides a visual representation of my Leadership Model.

In many of my seminars, I have asked participants "Which of the 3 Cs do leaders do most often?" The consistent answer is "challenge." A typical comment is "The leaders at my company are great at throwing out the challenges but they do nothing in the other Cs." One-dimensional leaders aren't effective. Leaders need to be proficient at doing all three Cs. In addition, it's important leaders understand the interrelationships among challenge, confidence, and coaching.

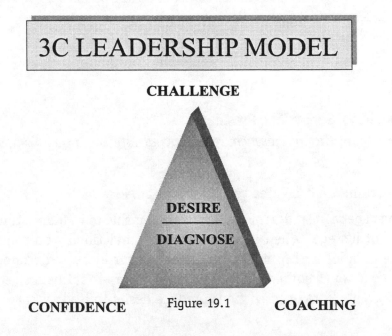

3C LEADERSHIP MODEL

CHALLENGE

DESIRE
—
DIAGNOSE

CONFIDENCE   Figure 19.1   **COACHING**

Here are several ways the 3-Cs are interconnected:

• Tough challenges often effect people's confidence.

• When people are trained and coached in how to apply new skills, they feel more prepared, more confident.

• As confidence increases people are willing to take on bigger and bigger challenges.

• Confident people clearly see the challenges in front of them. In addition, confident people aren't afraid to ask for help and guidance. (coaching)

Leaders provide what's needed to help people grow and develop.

The following three case studies describe how various leaders have applied the **3-C Leadership Model.** The leaders I interviewed were:

• Mike Hays, Senior Vice President, Investment Group, Massachusetts Mutual Life Insurance Company

• Ruth Branson, Senior Vice President, Human Resources, Shaw's Supermarkets

• Dan Kelly, Vice President, Transportation Business, International Fuel Cells

▲

Mike Hays, Senior Vice President,

Investment Group, Massachusetts Mutual Life Insurance Company

Question: What creates your desire to be a leader?

Hays: I get a great deal of satisfaction being able to influence things. Part of it's ego. When you have strong convictions, you want to take on a leadership role. If you believe your ideas and strategies are good for the organization, you willingly try to influence people and events. Strong convictions produce desire to lead.

Question: How do you diagnose what type of leadership an individual or group needs?

Hays: I look at two factors: the situation and the people involved. Situations that are familiar and straightforward often require a hands-off approach. A nudge here or there is all that's needed. In other cases where there's confusion and chaos and problems are unclear, I get much more involved in sorting out the issues.

As I work with people, I develop a good idea as to what style of leadership they need. People's needs do change. I directly involve people in the process and listen to what they have to say. Up front you have to take the time to communicate and understand their points of view, really listen to their ideas and concerns. A lot of managers spend thirty seconds listening and two hours talking. That ratio isn't conducive to figuring out how to help people be successful.

Question: What approach or techniques do you use to challenge people?

Hays: I candidly tell people what I know, what I believe, and why the challenge is important. People resist change. You need to help people get past the resistance so they are fully committed to the vision or goal.

Before I can challenge people, I need to be fully committed to the vision. If I'm not committed, I can't convince anyone else to step up to the challenge. I try to give people lots of information about the business challenge. Why is this action necessary? In addition, I respect people. I want to hear their concerns. Gaining people's buy-in and commitment to the challenge takes time and effort. What I don't want is people who agree with everything I say in the meeting but who deep down don't support the initiative.

Question: What approach or techniques do you use to build confidence in people?

Hays: I let people know I have confidence in them. Sometimes it's just a matter of telling people that they have the skills and motivation to succeed. Also, leaders have to demonstrate a willingness to take a chance on a person. You also have to stand by people when a situation doesn't go as planned.

Question: What approaches or techniques do you use to coach people?

Hays: I try to give people candid but tactful feedback. Coaching means helping people improve their performance. Without frequent and useful feedback, it's difficult to improve performance. I also recognize positive accomplishments.

Question: What connections or interrelationships do you see among challenge, confidence, and coaching?

Hays: They are pieces of the same puzzle. When people achieve a tough challenge, they feel more confident. When leaders coach people, they improve their current skills or gain new skills. This also makes people feel more confident. The 3 Cs support each other.

Question: What are the key skills leaders need to be effective and successful?

Hays: Honesty and integrity are critical. If people don't trust you, they won't follow you. In addition, if you're going to lead you must believe in a vision. You need a vision you're willing to fight for. Leaders have courage to stand up for what they believe.

Communication and interpersonal skills are also important. But honesty, integrity, courage, and belief in your vision are the foundation. If you lack those traits, it doesn't matter how effective you are at communicating.

▲

Ruth Branson
Senior Vice President, Shaw's Supermarkets

Question: What creates the desire in you to be a leader?

Branson: The desire comes from having a vision I believe in and want to share. A vision that requires people to think and act way beyond current reality gets me excited and energized. I also have a real love of developing people. Helping people exceed what they think they can accomplish is very rewarding, and with the leadership to guide them, it can become a reality.

Question: How do you diagnose what type of leadership an individual or group needs?

Branson: We use assessment centers and 360 feedback as ways to identify where people need help. [360 feedback means managers receive performance evaluations from all directions—up, down, and laterally. Direct reports, peers, customers, team members, and the boss provide separate assessments.] In our assessment centers participants go through a number of simulated events. Their behaviors and responses are compared to our "success profile" for their particular position or career path. We need managers who have the technical and interpersonal skills to be successful.

The 360 feedback lets people know how various constituents view their performance. This is valuable information. What I've found is some people may be very effective at managing their boss and peers but aren't as effective with their direct reports. Assessment centers and 360 feedback not only identify individual skill gaps but also point out organizational issues that need addressing.

Question: What approach and techniques do you use to challenge people?

Branson: Certainly a clearly stated vision is one way to challenge people. I also challenge people by assigning them to task forces. These are multidiscipline teams that are chartered to address companywide issues. Being part of these groups broadens people's thinking. Another way we challenge people is through cross-fertilization. We move people into new positions from one function to another, from line to staff, from a district to the corporate office. These job changes stretch people to see the business from new perspectives. We also challenge people to continue their formal education. We urge people to get M.B.A. degrees or, in some cases, complete their undergraduate degrees.

Question: What approaches and techniques do you use to build confidence in people?

Branson: I mentioned earlier that we frequently assign people to various task forces. On these assignments people often find that a lot of their competencies apply to company wide problems. When people realize that many of their skills are transferable, they feel more sure of the breadth of their abilities.

I always encourage people to make presentations. For example, if a human resource topic needs to be discussed at a board of directors meeting, I'll have one of my direct reports make the presentation. This gives them exposure to management and confidence in their skills.

The most important way we build confidence is through our mentoring program. Having a mentor with whom you can discuss problems and bounce ideas off of gives you a safety net. People are less afraid of getting out of their comfort zones if they know they have a mentor who will guide and support them. It is a nonthreatening relationship since mentors are not "bosses" who have control over raises or promotions.

Question: What approaches and techniques do you use to coach people?

Branson: Certainly our mentor program is one way we coach people. All of our high-potential employees have mentors who are at the vice president level or above. A good mentor is trained to be an effective coach and facilitator. We also use executive coaches. If an executive has a flaw in, say, managing conflict or is abrasive in managing change, we will hire an executive coach to work one-on-one with the individual.

Question: What connections or interrelationships do you see among challenge, confidence, and coaching?

Branson: They are closely related. Unless you have confidence, you won't accept a tough challenge. You gain confidence by developing technical and interpersonal skills. A lot of that skill development occurs through effective coaching and mentoring.

The 3-C Leadership Model makes it apparent that all three leadership actions—challenge, building confidence, and coaching—are equally important and each is a critical piece of the whole.

Question: What are the key skills and traits leaders need to be effective and successful?

Branson: I think leaders need the following:

Vision. Leaders need to know where the company is going. In addition, they need to be able to translate the vision into words that people can understand and get excited about.

Appreciation of People. The quality of the organization is determined by the quality of the people. Effective leaders appreciate people's talents and skills and stretch people to achieve their best.

Ability to Ask the Right Questions. The right question helps focus attention on the right issues. However, once the question is asked, leaders must listen and take the time needed to fully understand other people's ideas and opinions.

Effective Communication. Leaders have to write and speak in a way that's clear and compelling. The ability to get people excited and willing to follow you has a lot to do with how effective you communicate your message.

Intelligence. Leaders need the ability to interpret and process lots of information. Being able to connect the dots and see patterns in a rapidly changing business world is critical.

Commitment. Leaders must demonstrate the desire and determination needed to achieve their vision. If the leader isn't fully committed, how can you expect others to go the extra mile?

Dan Kelly
Vice President, Transportation Business, International Fuel Cells

Question: What creates the desire in you to be a leader?

Kelly: I think I was born with it. I love the challenges required to succeed. I get a great deal of satisfaction helping people develop. You have to be willing to challenge people and hold them accountable for results. People who only want to be buddies with everyone won't challenge people or give them candid feedback. Desire also comes from being committed to your vision.

Question: How do you diagnose what type of leadership an individual or team needs?

Kelly: I try not to prejudge people in terms of what they can or can't accomplish. I've been very surprised on occasion at what some people have accomplished. I believe in setting clear expectations and supporting people as required. As teams and individuals give me feedback on their progress, I get clues and indications of what's needed in terms of leadership. However, before I provide any guidance or advice, I require the team members to have their own recommendations to solve their problem. I don't want to own their problem. Effective leaders figure out what the organization needs and what people need to be successful.

Question: What approach or techniques do you use to challenge people?

Kelly: Before you can challenge people they need self-confidence. They need to believe that they can be successful. Last week I told one of my managers that he needed to develop a technology plan that no one in the company knows how to accomplish. Breakthrough thinking—that's a challenge. People don't accept that type of challenge if they lack confidence.

I believe one of my key roles is to develop people. The way I develop people is by challenging them with tough goals and new mountains to climb. Most people have more potential than they realize.

Question: What approaches and techniques do you use to build confidence in people?

Kelly: I begin with trust. Trust is critical. Before I can build someone's confidence, I need to trust them. When we establish project expectations, I try to weave into the conversation that the person has the talents and abilities to be successful. But it's more than just words. It's the trust I have in them and the way I deliver the message that shows my confidence. I also tell people that if they make a mistake I will support their decisions. I try never to attack people for making decisions. That creates fear and when people are afraid, that leads to inaction, and inaction is not acceptable.

Question: What approaches and techniques do you use to coach people?

Kelly: Individuals and teams must provide me with periodic updates, usually once per week. Our meetings provide teaching moments. I'm very willing to discuss and give guidance on their recommendations. I don't want upward delegation. I want to hear their ideas. Coaching often involves helping people learn new ways to see a problem and all the impacts of their recommendation.

I also give people frequent opportunities to make presentations to customers and senior management. These are often significant emotional events and powerful learning opportunities. After the presentation we discuss what was positive and negative. What could they do differently to be more effective? People appreciate the feedback. Part of coaching is encouraging people to try new, hopefully more effective, ways of communicating their ideas.

Question: What connections or interrelationships do you see among challenge, confidence, and coaching?

Kelly: They are tightly woven. Challenge is needed to make people develop. But before people accept new challenges, they need confidence. They need to believe they can be successful. Effective coaches build people's confidence and challenge them to climb to the next level.

A lot of leaders don't provide effective coaching. They simply pass on customer demands, which are often the tough challenges. Without coaching and confidence, people flounder.

Question: What are the key skills leaders need to be effective and successful?

Kelly: I think leaders need the following skills and traits:

Ability to Set the Example. Leaders need to have confidence in themselves. They must believe in their vision and show the organization how committed they are to achieving success. If you don't set the example, you lack credibility. Without credibility, you can't influence anyone.

Ability to Motivate. Leaders must connect with people in a way that they become excited about the vision and challenges they face.

Decisiveness. Leaders need to make decisions in a timely manner. Being decisive requires confidence to take risks and commitment to achieving your vision.

Trust. Leaders must trust and empower people. Don't micromanage. Make people responsible for a whole project—not just a task.

Involvement. Leaders need to be visible and involved in what people are thinking and doing. In addition, leaders need to involve people in all aspects of the business.

Stability. Leaders can't be overly emotional when business success or setbacks occur. My motto is "never too high and never too low." When problems "hit the fan," employees look to the leader as a role model to follow.

Good Communication. Leaders need to provide honest, frequent, and factual information in a way that motivates people. Leaders who relate to their audience have the best chance of communicating their message.

Ability to Develop People. Leaders get people to do tasks that are unfamiliar and scary. They believe people have untapped abilities. They unlock hidden potentials.

Constancy in the Organization. Leaders have a clearly defined purpose and set of goals. Their vision doesn't change daily. People understand where the leaders are going and their strategy for getting there.

PART VI
Leadership Development

Your leadership style should reflect your special gifts and talents. Observe and learn from other leaders but don't copy them. Perfect your own, unique style.

If you never take risks and challenge your "comfort zone," you'll never know what you can achieve. The biggest challenge is not out there in the marketplace but is the journey you find in yourself. When you face difficult challenges and step up to lead, the biggest prize is the following:

- You shape the future.

- You help others achieve their potential.

- You attain courage, self-knowledge and self-confidence.

Challenge the boundaries you set for yourself. Don't lose your zest for adventure, for taking a risk, for doing something that hasn't been done before. Be curious. The greatest waste of our natural resources is the number of people who never try to reach their potential. Arthur C. Clarke said that the only way of discovering the limits of the possible is to venture a little way past them into the impossible.

Leadership development occurs at three levels.

1. Finding your internal light and letting it glow. Leadership starts in the heart and soul.

2. Developing you character and values.

3. Strengthening your knowledge and skills. Execution requires "know how."

Developing your leadership talents is a life-long journey. Below is a list of suggestions and resources that can help you along the way. However, action is required. Note: no successful person has been described as being long on philosophy and short on implementation. Follow the "practice-feedback-revisions" cycle until you perfect your leadership skills.

- **Reflection**—Spend some time each week in reflection and meditation. Focus on the big, philosophical questions such as, "What's your passion?" "What are your core values and beliefs?" "What's your mission as a leader?" "How are you challenging yourself?" "What adjectives do you want people to use when describing your leadership style?"

- **Proactive**—Leaders are proactive. Get in the habit of predicting the future. What will happen next week? Next month? Track your predictions. How accurate are you? What factors or trends did you miss? Strive to identify patterns and understand the principles behind the behavior.

- **Leadership Stories**—Leaders often tell stories to explain who they are, what they believe in and where they are going. What's your story? Describe a "defining moment" in your life? How has this shaped your beliefs and values? Practice telling your story until it's focused, clear and inspiring.

- **Self-Evaluation**—Take time to evaluate your leadership skills. Complete the "Be the Leader Survey" that appears in the Appendix section of this book. Identify your top three strengths and three areas needing improvement. What actions can you take to build on your strengths and reduce your weaknesses?

- **Standard of Excellence**—Set a goal to pursue a standard of excellence in some area of your life. Gain the experience of what it takes and feels like to be the "best." Where do you normally set your goals? Do "fear of failure" or "fear of success" hold you back?

- **360 Feedback**—It's important to receive regular feedback from a variety of people including bosses, customers, peers, team members, and direct reports. You don't have to agree with their feedback, but at least consider it. In the appendix section, there are several questions you can ask people with whom you work.

- **Mentors**—Find and utilize mentors. They provide you with information you won't learn in a textbook. The big question in selecting a mentor is: Can you learn from this person? Does the individual have the character, attitudes, accomplishments and leadership experiences you admire? Is the person interested in helping you?

- **Interviews**—Interview leaders you admire. Be curious. What career path did they follow? What were their most significant learning experiences? What would they do differently?

- **Authentic self-expression**—I include honesty and integrity as "must have" qualities in a leader. Try being totally honest and direct whenever you speak. Don't try to please people or "sugar-coat" the message. Be genuine. Read *Leadership from the Inside Out: Seven Pathways to Mastery* by Kevin Cashman

- **Self-confidence**—Write down the five accomplishments that have had the most impact on your self-confidence. Keep a running list of your significant achievements. Review it at least once a month.

- **Education**—There are many college courses and degree programs that focus on leadership. The following web sites provides useful information about college programs.

  gradschools.com

  leadersandleadership.com

- **Online Education**—Check out the following web sites. These sites have good articles and other resources to develop your leadership knowledge and skills.

emergingleader.com	mgeneral.com
energizeinc.com	perdidomagazine.com
iofl.org	refresher.com
leadershipnow.com	smartleadership.com
leader-values.com	tompeters.com
managementfirst.com	

- **Seminars**—There are many good seminars that focus on management and leadership topics. The following organizations offer leadership seminars:

  American Management Association

  Center for Creative Leadership

  SkillPath

  Be the Leader Associates (My company)

- **Books/Magazines/Journals**—Certainly there are many excellent resources that provide articles and advice on leadership. Some to consider include:

  Across the Board

  Fast Company

  Harvard Business Review

  Harvard Management Communication Update

  Industry Week

  Leader to Leader

  Leadership Journal

- **Audiotapes**—No time to read? Audio-Tech Business Book Summaries is an excellent resource for audiotapes focused on business books and leadership topics. Here are a few examples

    Bringing Out the Best in People By Aubrey Daniels

    The Will to Lead By Marvin Bower

    The 7 Habits of Highly Effective People By Stephen R. Covey

    Jack Welch and the GE Way By Robert Slater

    The Power of Simplicity By Jack Trout and Steve Rivkin

- **Coach**—Volunteer to coach an athletic team. This is great experience to perfect your management and leadership skills. It provides real practice in challenging players, building their confidence and coaching to improve their skills.

Summary—Leadership Development

All journeys start with thinking, planning, and then execution. Developing your leadership potential requires focused time and dedication in each area. No, you can't develop your leadership skills in one minute or one year. It's a lifetime of exciting work. The important thing is to get started. Think, plan, implement and learn as you go.

Final Thoughts

My challenge to you regarding the 3 Cs:

Challenge

- Help people achieve their dreams. Help people become more and achieve more than they ever thought possible.

- Set high standards; be demanding. Expect more than others think is possible.

- Set the example. Take risks, get out of your own comfort zone.

Confidence

- Look for and find the hidden talents in yourself and others.

- Build people up, don't tear them down. Remind people of their best performance, not their worst.

- Drive out fear. Focus on the possibilities, not the obstacles.

Coaching

- Treat every interaction with others as a chance to be both coach and student.

- Benchmark. Point out examples of great performance. Provide candid and helpful feedback.

- Set the example. Be curious. Keep learning and growing.

If not you, who?
If not now, when?

— Abraham Maslow

Let the leaders step forward!

APPENDIX

The purpose of this appendix is to provide a survey instrument to help you evaluate your leadership skills. The "Be The Leader Survey" focuses on the seven major aspects of the **3-C Leadership Model**. The survey is a self-evaluation tool. However, if on the survey you change "I" to "your name," it could be completed by others such as bosses, peers, team members, customers, and direct reports.

Be the Leader Survey

Directions: Take time to think about and reflect on each question. Circle the number that best describes you.

1	2	3	4	5
Never	Seldom	Sometimes	Usually	Always

I. Desire To Lead

I want to lead.	1	2	3	4	5
I like taking risks.	1	2	3	4	5
I volunteer to be the first to learn and do new tasks.	1	2	3	4	5
People describe me as being "passionate and determined."	1	2	3	4	5
I take a personal role in trying to change things for the better.	1	2	3	4	5
I step forward and take charge in leaderless situations.	1	2	3	4	5

II. Diagnosing What People Need

I see things the way they are, not how I wish they were.	1	2	3	4	5
I am able to determine people's strengths and weaknesses.	1	2	3	4	5
I carefully listen to what people say.	1	2	3	4	5
I carefully observe people.	1	2	3	4	5
I find unique relationships between people and events.	1	2	3	4	5
I change my diagnosis based on new information.	1	2	3	4	5
I'm able to separate symptoms from underlying problems.	1	2	3	4	5
People describe me as "knowing exactly what to say or do."	1	2	3	4	5

III. Challenging the Status Quo

I consistently set high standards.	1	2	3	4	5
I encourage dreaming and thinking outside the box.	1	2	3	4	5
I see possibilities where none seem to exist.	1	2	3	4	5
I have a vision.	1	2	3	4	5
I require people to continuously improve their performance.	1	2	3	4	5
I set goals that stretch people.	1	2	3	4	5
I ask questions that challenge current methods and procedures.	1	2	3	4	5

1	2	3	4	5
Never	**Seldom**	**Sometimes**	**Usually**	**Always**

IV. Building Confidence

I am an optimistic person who sees the positive side of situations (the cup is half full).   1   2   3   4   5

I reward and recognize people for good or improved performance.   1   2   3   4   5

I encourage people to believe in themselves.   1   2   3   4   5

I instill competence and capability in others.   1   2   3   4   5

I affirm people's talents, abilities, and potential.   1   2   3   4   5

People describe me as a leader who assigns responsibility and authority.   1   2   3   4   5

V. Coaching

I consistently set high standards.   1   2   3   4   5

Other people come to me for advice and guidance.   1   2   3   4   5

I am able to motivate people.   1   2   3   4   5

I am able to explain what to do and how to do it.   1   2   3   4   5

People describe me as a good coach/teacher.   1   2   3   4   5

I provide effective and timely performance feedback.   1   2   3   4   5

I regularly seek and accept feedback from others about my behavior.   1   2   3   4   5

VI. Communicating

I think through my purpose before I communicate.   1   2   3   4   5

I use words that are precise and understood by the receiver.   1   2   3   4   5

My messages are organized and easy to follow.   1   2   3   4   5

When listening, I make eye contact with the speaker.   1   2   3   4   5

I listen for the main ideas and supporting points.   1   2   3   4   5

People describe me as being a "good listener."   1   2   3   4   5

VII. Influencing Others to Follow

I am able to sell my ideas.   1   2   3   4   5

I demonstrate great passion and commitment.   1   2   3   4   5

People describe me as "being influential."   1   2   3   4   5

I have credibility; people believe what I say.   1   2   3   4   5

People know I'm concerned with their needs and point of view.   1   2   3   4   5

People ask me to be the leader.   1   2   3   4   5

Summarizing Results

Once you have completed the survey, average your scores for each of the seven major sections.

I.   Desiring to Lead   _____

II.   Diagnosing What People Need.   _____

III. Challenging the Status Quo   _____

IV.   Building Confidence   _____

V.   Coaching   _____

VI.   Communicating   _____

VII. Influencing Others to Follow   _____

What are your strengths, (4.0 and higher) and areas needing improvement, (3.9 and lower)? Are there questions you answered, "Never", or "Seldom?" What are the implications? What knowledge, skills or motivation are needed?

Self-assessments are important. Equally important is receiving feedback from other people such as customers, bosses, peers, mentors, team members, and direct reports. Every six months or so ask five to seven trusted individuals for their feedback. Possible questions to ask include:

- What should I be doing "more of" and "less of" in each of the seven survey areas?

- What are my greatest strengths? Areas needing improvement?

- In what situations should I take more of a leadership role?

BIBLIOGRAPHY

Aguayo, R. *Dr. Deming: The Man Who Taught the Japanese about Quality*. 1st ed.New York: Simon & Schuster, 1990.

Ash, M. K. *Mary Kay on People Management*. 1st ed. New York: Warner Books, 1984.

Bardwick, J. M. *Danger in the Comfort Zone*. 2nd ed. New York: Amacom, 1995.

Bennis, W., and B. Nanus. *Leaders*. 1st ed. New York: Harper and Row, 1985.

Blank, W. *The 9 Natural Laws of Leadership*. 1st ed. New York: Amacom, 1995.

Branden, N. *Self-Esteem at Work*. 1st ed. San Francisco: Jossey-Bass Publishers, 1998.

Canfield, J., and J. Miller. *Heart at Work*. 1st ed. New York: McGraw Hill, 1996.

Case, J. "A Company of Business People." *Inc.* (April 1993).

Caudron, S. "Teach Downsizing Survivors How to Thrive." *Personnel Journal* (January 1996).

Cohen, H. "The Performance Paradox." *The Academy of Management Executive* (August 1998).

Conger, J. "The Necessary Art of Persuasion." *Harvard Business Review* (May–June 1998).

Csikszentmihaly, M. *Flow*. 1st ed. New York: Harper Collins Publishers.

David, G. "We Are Engaged in a Giant Contest with the Outside World." *UTCWorld* (June 1998).

Depree, M. *Leadership Jazz*. 1st ed. New York: Doubleday, 1992.

Eitel, C. *Eitel Time Turnaround Secrets*. 1st ed. Orlando, Fla.: Harcourt Brace and Company, 1995.

Eitel, C. *Mapping Your Legacy*. 1st ed. Atlanta, Ga.: Peregrinzilla Press, 1998.

Farkas, C., and P. DeBacker. *Maximum Leadership*. 1st ed. New York: Henry Holt and Company, 1996.

Georges, J. C. "The Myth of Soft-Skills Training." *Training* (January 1996).

Gilbert, P. B. *The Eleven Commandments of Wildly Successful Women*. 1st ed. New York: Macmillan Spectrum, 1996.

Heifetz, R. A., and D. L. Laurie. "The Work of Leadership." *Harvard Business Review* (January–February 1997).

Hesselbein, F., M. Goldsmith, and R. Beckhard. *The Leader of the Future*. 1st ed. San Francisco: Jossey-Bass Publishers, 1996.

Johnson, P. "Reebok Executive Champions Constant Improvement," *Sunday Republican* (April 26, 1998).

Jones, L. B. *Jesus, CEO: Using Ancient Wisdom for Visionary Leadership*. 1st ed. New York: Hyperion, 1995.

Jones, M. *Creating an Imaginative Life*. 1st ed. Berkeley, Calif.: Conari Press, 1995.

Kotter, J. *Leading Change*. 1st ed. Cambridge, Ma.: Harvard University Press, 1996.

Kouzes, J. M., and B. Z. Posner. *The Leadership Challenge*. 2nd ed. San Francisco: Jossey-Bass Publishers, 1995.

Krapek, K., "To the People of Pratt & Whitney," <u>Directions</u> (special edition 1996).

Kriegel, R. J., and L. Patter. *If It Ain't Broke....Break It*. 1st ed. New York: Warner Books, 1996.

Labich, Kenneth. "Sometimes the Sky Is Falling." *Fortune*. (October 14, 1996).

Leach, L. "TQM, Re-engineering, and the Edge of Chaos." *Quality Progress* (February 1996).

McClenahen, J. "52 Fiefdoms No More." *Industry Week* (January 20, 1997).

McCormick, J. "The Vision Thing:Try it, You'll Like It." *Business Month* (May 1990).

Miller, J. "Argue with Success." *Business Horizons* (November–December 1995).

Plenert, G. *World-Class Manager*. 1st ed. Rocklin, Calif.: Prima Publishing, 1995.

Riley, P. *The Winner Within*. 1st ed. New York: G. P. Putnam & Sons, 1993.

Schaffer, R. H. "Demand Better Results—And Get Them." *Harvard Business Review* (March–April 1991).

Shechtman, M. *Working without a Net*. 1st ed. New York: Pocket Books, 1994.

Sherman, Strat S. "Stretch Goals: The Dark Side of Asking for Miracles." *Fortune* (November 1995).

Smith, M. R. *Contrarian Management*. 1st ed. New York: Amacom, 1992.

Stack, Jack. *The Great Game of Business*. 1st ed. New York: Bantam Doubleday Dell, 1994.

Summitt, P., with S. Jenkins. *Reach for the Summit*. 1st ed. New York: Broadway Books, 1998.

Thornton, P. B. *Lessons from the Best Managers*. 1st ed. Morrisville, Pa.: International Information Associates, 1991.

Thornton, P. B. "Teamwork: Focus, Frame, Facilitate." *Management Review* (November 1992).

Thornton, P. B. *The Answers Are on the Office Wall*. 1st ed. Exeter, N.H.: Monochrome Press, 1994.

Tichy, Noel M., with Eli Cohen *The Leadership Engine*. 1st ed. New York: HarperCollins Publishers, 1997.

Tichy, Noel M., and S. Sherman. "Jack Welch's Lessons for Success." *Fortune* (January 25, 1993).

Tully, S. "Why Go for Stretch Targets." *Fortune* (November 14, 1994).

Verespej, M. A. "Growth by Design." *Industry Week* (January 8, 1996).

Wah, L. "Transforming Human Resources around the World." (AMA Report) *Management Review* (July/August 1998).

Werner, T., and R. Lynch. *The Consultant's Handbook*. 1st ed. Littleton, CO.: Qual Team, Inc.

Wheatley, Margaret. *Leadership and the New Science*. 1st ed. San Francisco: Berrett-Koehler, 1992.

Zenke, R. "The Corporate Coach." *Training* (December 1996).

Other Research

Interviews and discussions were held with the following leaders:

Dr. Tony Allessandra, keynote speaker and author of *Charisma* and *The Platinum Rule*.

Judy Batchelor, Manager, Software Quality Assurance, Otis Elevator, Division of United Technologies, Inc.

Phil Beaudoin, Leadership Trainer/Oganizational Development Consultant

Steve Bennett, Manager, Quality, International Fuel Cells

Tony Borgen, Technical Specialist—Quality Systems, Hamilton Standard, Division of United Technologies, Inc.

Ruth Branson, Senior Vice President, Human Resources, Shaw's Supermarkets

Steve Chanin, Director, Operations, Asea Brown Boveri

Tony Choma, Manager, Drafting, Hamilton Standard, Division of United Technologies, Inc.

Bill Cox, former Vice President, Human Resources, Dexter Corporation

Stefani Cummings, Benefits Manager, Hamilton Standard, Division of United Technologies, Inc.

Tricia Day, Chief Labor Relations Officer, Massachusetts Bay Transportation Authority

Robert DeRoy, Controller, Dynamic Controls/HS, Inc.

Janice Deskus, Vice President, Training and Quality Implementation, CIGNA Health Care

Charlie Eitel, President and Chief Operating Officer, Interface, Inc.

Jay Goltz, President, Artist's Frame Service

Mike Hays, Senior Vice President, Investment Group, Mass Mutual Insurance Co.

Michael Z. Kay, President and CEO, LSG Sky Chefs, Inc.

Dan Kelly, Vice President, Transportation Business, International Fuel Cells

Marlin Knight, Manager, Human Resources, Hamilton Standard, Space Systems International

Robert La Palme, Chief Financial Officer, Jen-Coat, Inc.

Ayn La Plant, President, Beekley Corporation

Sue Lewis, Executive Vice President and Chief Real Estate Officer, The Travelers

Jim Ligotti, Global Product Manager, Carrier Corporation

Frank Maguire, President, Hearth Communications Group

Vin Misciagna, Director, General Aviation, Hamilton Standard, Division of United Technologies, Inc.

John Nicoletta, Leadership Trainer, Organizational Development Consultant

Steve Pavlech, Manager, Operations Strategic Planning, Hamilton Standard, Division of United Technologies, Inc.

Tom Phillips, former President, Dynamic Controls/HS, Inc.

Rob Porro, Leadership Associate, Hamilton Standard, Division of United Technologies, Inc.

Chris Poythress, Director, Engineering, Hamilton Standard, Space Systems International

Donna Shaw, Contracts Manager, Dynamic Controls/HS, Inc.

Wayne Spock, Manager, Engineering, Hamilton Standard, Division of United Technologies, Inc.

Don Sweet, Vice President, Finance, Siebe Pneumatics

Mary Jean Thornton, President, Busy B Ice Cream

John Thorpe, Director, Staffing, AGDATA

ACKNOWLEDGMENTS

I would like to thank the following people:

Mary Jean, Kate, and Andy for your support and encouragement.

Donna DeCaro Conley, Mary Jean Thornton, Stephani Cummings, John Nicoletta, Vin Misciagna, Marlin Knight, Tony Borgen, Dick Knight, Chris Wiernicki, and Phil Graham for providing various examples, stories, and anecdotes.

Dr. Neil Yeager, Dr. Deborah Barnhart, Professor M. J. Thornton, Bob Glennon, and John Mayo for reading my manuscript and providing valuable advice, guidance, and feedback.

Phil Beaudoin and John Nicoletta for helping me design the Be The Leader survey.

Clare Daniels for typing and retyping my manuscript more times than I care to remember.

Nancy Hall for editing my manuscript and providing ideas on how to organize topics and chapters.

Kate Thornton for editing the second edition.

Patty Deyo for designing the cover and several figures.

ABOUT THE AUTHOR

Paul B. Thornton is a managing partner in the consulting firm "Be the Leader Associates." His company specializes in designing and delivering programs aimed at leadership development. Throughout his career, he has been involved in the selection and development of leaders. His background includes experience in the following:

- Strategic planning
- Succession planning
- Management assessment centers
- Programs to identify and develop high-potential employees
- Teaching management and leadership skills

Over the past twenty-five years he has trained more than seven thousand supervisors and managers on how to be more effective leaders. Paul has conducted leadership training programs for Management Development International, Kuwait Oil Corporation, and United Technologies Corporation. He has written numerous articles on management and leadership as well as two books, *Lessons from the Best Managers* and *The Answers Are on the Office Wall*. He's been a full-time and part-time faculty member at several colleges. While at American International College, he was also the varsity hockey coach. He compiled a record of 65 wins and 33 losses over four years.

At the undergraduate level he studied psychology and political science while attending Ohio University. He has a Master of Business Administration degree from American International College and a Master of Education degree from Suffolk University.

Paul B. Thornton conducts seminars on leadership and presents a keynote speech titled "Be the Leader, Make the Difference."

To contact Be the Leader Asssociates
phone: (413)569-9835
fax: (413)598-0870
web site: www.betheleader.com

Be The Leader Associates

We help companies select and develop great leaders.

Our Approach

We work with senior management to establish a "Leadership Success Profile" for their company. Additional steps in our process include assessing current leaders, determining needs, creating and implementing development plans, and evaluating results.

Services

- Leadership Assessments
- Development Planning
- Executive Coaching
- Leadership Training
- Rotational Programs
- Leadership Retreats

Seminars

- Be the Leader, Make the Difference
- Dealing with Difficult People
- Situational Leadership Theory
- Performance Management
- ABC's of Motivation
- Conducting Great Meetings